# Reweaving the Fabric

# REWEAVING THE FABRIC

How Congregations and
Communities Can Come Together
To Build Their Neighborhoods

RONALD E. NORED, SR.

Black Belt Press
Montgomery

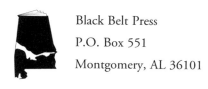

Black Belt Press
P.O. Box 551
Montgomery, AL 36101

Copyright © 1999 by Ronald E. Nored, Sr.
All rights reserved under International and Pan-American Copyright Conventions. Published in the United States by Black Belt Press, a division of Black Belt Publishing, LLC, Montgomery, Alabama.

**Library of Congress Cataloging-in-Publication Data**
Nored, Ronald E. (Ronald Eugene), 1960-
   Reweaving the fabric: how congregations and communities can come together to build their neighborhoods / Ronald E. Nored, Sr.
      p. cm.
   Includes bibliographical references and index.
   ISBN 1-881320-50-2
      1. Urban renewal—Alabama—Birmingham.  2. Community development, Urban—Alabama-Birmingham. 3. City churches—Alabama—Birmingham. 4. Church and social problems—Alabama—Birmingham. I. Title.
HT177.B57N67 1999
307'.09761'781—dc21                                      98-54368
                                                          CIP

Design by Randall Williams
Printed in the United States of America

*The Black Belt, defined by its dark, rich soil, stretches across central Alabama. It was the heart of the cotton belt. It was and is a place of great beauty, of extreme wealth and grinding poverty, of pain and joy. Here we take our stand, listening to the past, looking to the future.*

*To My Beloved Sons*

Ronald Jr., Randall James, and R. Christopher Nored

# CONTENTS

# Foreword

REVEREND Ronald Nored's book, *Reweaving the Fabric,* is a documentation of how concerned citizens can cause a miracle to happen. We read in Reverend Nored's own words the actual day-to-day transformation of a poor, decaying slum neighborhood into a thriving, attractive place for families to live, work and play.

During my sojourn with Martin Luther King, Jr., we began to see poverty as disabling as racism. We believed that as segregation was immoral in a democracy, poverty was immoral in a nation as wealthy as the United States of America.

The book reflects on how neighbors can come together in an Olympian effort to aid each other and save a community.

Peace and blessings,

ANDREW YOUNG

# Preface

PASTORS and other community leaders all over the country are constantly flooded with reminders about how so many of our neighborhoods and communities, both urban and rural, are in the midst of devastating social and economic crises. News reports fill our television screens and our mailboxes. They leave in our minds one urgent question, "What can we do?"

This book, *Reweaving the Fabric,* is about answering that question. It shows us how we can use our hands to rebuild community rather than wringing them or pointing defensively at one another. We can use our minds for more than figuring out ways to keep our churches healthy in the middle of neighborhoods that are suffering and in danger of dying. We can use our mouths to issue invitations to new partnerships between congregational members and neighborhood residents, between neighborhoods long separated by the active legacies of race and class, and ultimately between God and all the people created to live together in the places we call cities and communities.

I am obviously pleased that Bethel A.M.E. Church and the Reverend Ronald Nored, pastor and author, are at the heart of this story. This fact both encourages and challenges all our churches. But I urge leaders from every religious tradition and every type of neighborhood to read the following pages carefully and to search for your own role in making the kind of story told here more common than the other kinds of stories we hear so often about our neighborhoods today. I am convinced that God is calling us to that work in all our congregations and communities—and that there is a way for us to get on with that work starting right now. I trust that if you are not convinced of that statement already, you will be by the time you finish reading *Reweaving the Fabric*.

Peace, Power, Love,

JOHN HURST ADAMS

Senior Bishop, African Methodist Episcopal Church
Founder and Chair Emeritus, Congress of National Black Churches

# Introduction

### REV. ROBERT MONTGOMERY
**Greater Birmingham Ministries**

IN THE fall of 1990, the six-block neighborhood in the Ensley section of Birmingham Alabama known as Sandy Bottom was filled with decaying, substandard, shotgun-style houses. The utility lines leading to the houses drooped down to within five feet of the ground in many yards. Everywhere there were trash-filled, vacant lots scattered throughout the neighborhood. The streets were narrow and often muddy from lack of adequate drainage sewers. Residents were daily troubled by drug traffic, economic decline, absentee landlords, and inadequate social services. Sandy Bottom's residents had all but given up hope for this historic, but now dying, neighborhood.

In the fall of 1996, the same six-block neighborhood, renamed Sandy Vista, saw the completion of the thirtieth new home on its recently widened streets, streets that now boasted new curbs and drainage sewers. Newly installed sidewalks are well-lit by modern street lights, and the last of the shotgun homes has been demolished to make way for the next house in the sixty-four home development. Residents are now homeowners and members of the Sandy Vista Residents Association, the organization primarily responsible for making all decisions about the future of the neighborhood.

Where once neighbors gathered to mourn the death of their community, now they gather regularly to plan how to revitalize a commercial district adjacent to their revitalized neighborhood. Where once the sound of children's voices had all but been silenced, now there are bicycles and tricycles parked in nearly every driveway. Long-time residents now mingle with the new arrivals and keep a watchful eye on the whole neighborhood from the front porches of their newly built corner residences. Where once distrust and worry prevailed among the residents, now there is a sense of hope, pride, and fierce optimism about the future.

What happened? This book tells the story of how a neighborhood, a church, and the surrounding community came together to change an area that nearly everyone was ready to write off as hopeless. This book is the story of how a neighborhood called Sandy Bottom became Sandy Vista. As they say in Sandy Bottom, "If it can happen here, it can happen anywhere."

The previously despairing residents of this Ensley neighborhood have been empowered to change their lives, to make their own decisions about their neighborhood, and to participate in developing and maintaining their community. The results have been surprising, even to those who believed good things could happen when people came together around a common vision of service and community revitalization. Ensley will never be the same, and the people who have lived through the Bethel Ensley Action Task (BEAT) experience in this community fully believe that the same kind of hope can be recovered in other neighborhoods in trouble.

This book is offered to other communities in that belief. We invite you to hear the story of the people of Sandy Bottom and the Bethel Ensley Action Task. It is a story of a journey toward rebuilding the fabric of community through new relationships of trust, listening, and caring. It is a journey toward community. It is a profoundly spiritual story and a very earthly one. The people of this neighborhood believe that they have seen God at work because they have a new relationship with one another so powerful that it has transformed a whole community.

# Acknowledgments

WRITING this book has provided me with a constant reminder of how utterly dependent I am upon God for all that I attempt to do. God's presence has been made known to me in very real ways through the contributors to this manuscript.

I am especially grateful to the Rev. Robert Montgomery for expending such extraordinary time reviewing, editing, expanding, and encouraging the completion of this document. Special thanks must also be paid to the Rev. Angela Hope Wright for putting on the finishing touches. Your commitment and approach to social justice has been inspiring.

I owe much gratitude to Bishops Frank Madison Reid Jr., Cornelius Egbert Thomas, and Zedekiah Lazett Grady for your Godly judgment in appointing me to serve as pastor of Bethel African Methodist Episcopal Church, Ensley (Birmingham), Alabama.

TO THE members of Bethel, I can only say that my life and ministry will never be the same because of your great love for the church and its mission. I have learned much from you about myself, God, and what it means to be a pastor in these challenging days. I am also most grateful to the residents of Sandy Bottom (now Sandy Vista) and board members of B.E.A.T.

And Greater Birmingham Ministries, I am indebted to you for the exceeding joy and purpose you have added to my life. Bonita Anderson, field representative for the Campaign for Human Development (CHD), thanks so much for being a friend and advocate for nearly a decade. CHD's contribution to our work in Ensley will never be forgotten.

Clarence Brown and Richard "Dick" Pigford, as a result of your stern commitment, great faith, and untiring quest for justice, a miracle has been wrought in Sandy Bottom. Thanks for believing in me and our vision of positive change in Ensley.

To our small, but efficient staff—Henry Scruggs, Davetta Brown, Lisa Williams, and Rev. Angie Wright—you have been "the wind beneath my wings."

Special appreciation also goes to the Christopher Reynolds Foundation, Mary Reynolds Babcock Foundation, Greater Birmingham Foundation, Robert Meyers and Hugh Kaul Foundation; thanks for your tremendous support.

Mayor Richard Arrington, you have always been one of my heroes. Thanks for taking a chance on this neighborhood-based effort.

To the countless volunteers and financial supporters, your labors and contributions have not been in vain.

Randall Williams, publisher of Black Belt Press, thanks for making this document possible. You have enabled this dream to be realized.

And, finally, to my wonderful wife, Linda, thanks for your enduring love and faith.

# Reweaving the Fabric

# 1

## Where We Started: At the Bottom

IT IS AN all too common story in today's inner cities: a neighborhood abandoned by the larger community. In this case, the situation was painfully summarized by one of my church members, who told me, "Reverend Nored, I am so ashamed by where I live I told my daughter never to bring my grandchildren to see me, because I don't want them to see me living like this. It's awful down here." Seventy-year-old Lelita Patton was right. The neighborhood where she lived, called Sandy Bottom, a six-block area surrounding Bethel African Methodist Episcopal Church in Birmingham's Ensley community, was in desperate shape.

Ms. Patton, who lived in one of the many extremely dilapidated shotgun houses in the neighborhood, was not alone in her dismay. Sandy Bottom had long been one of Birmingham's toughest neighborhoods. I remember Patricia Beals, a forty-eight-year-old lifelong resident of Ensley, saying to me, "When I was a child this community was a scary place. Most of the parents would not allow their children down here because it was very dangerous. My mother told us, 'Never, never go to Sandy Bottom.'"

Sandy Bottom was one of the most poverty-stricken neighborhoods in Birmingham. For nearly fifty years, the church had been the only viable institution in Sandy Bottom. Many members of Bethel AME had once

In the early 1990s, shotgun houses such as this one were common in the former "Sandy Bottom" neighborhood. Many of these houses had metal bars on their windows, holes in their floors, and very antiquated heating and cooling systems and plumbing facilities.

lived in Sandy Bottom, but as their economic status improved, they moved to more prosperous neighborhoods.

When I came to Birmingham to pastor Bethel A.M.E. Church in 1987, Sandy Bottom was indeed a very tough neighborhood. Many very low-income senior citizens lived in the neighborhood, and they had to contend with transients, drug dealers, and bootleggers. Few residents had any relationship to the church. For most in Sandy Bottom, neighborhood pride and hope had become foreign concepts.

Dilapidated shotgun houses like Mrs. Patton's made up Sandy Bottom's substandard housing stock. Lots were overgrown and filled with trash. The infrastructure was sorely inadequate. On rainy days, water covered the front yards due to poor sewer and drainage systems. There were no sidewalks, curbs or gutters. Utility lines hung literally at eye level, so you had to duck your head to walk from yard to yard. Absentee landlords were hard to track down and even harder to deal with.

The conditions in Sandy Bottom were not isolated. Ensley, once one of

Birmingham's most thriving communities, had become one of the city's "dying neighborhoods." The Ensley Works, a huge steel plant that once employed fifteen thousand, shut down in the early 1970s. That shutdown signaled a slow death for Ensley.

Once-thriving businesses in the community closed. Whole sections of the nearby retail area became vacant. Real estate prices plunged. Absentee landlords and landowners had little stake in the community. Shortsighted tax and property ordinances made it easy for landowners to let their properties decline. Houses and other buildings could not be sold for a profit, so owners simply cut their losses any way they could. They rented their property but generally made no improvements and provided no maintenance. Many owners all but abandoned their properties. The most they would do was to board them up after repeated complaints from neighbors and citations from the City. Delinquent taxes on dilapidated buildings made properties even more unattractive for new investors.

By 1990, Sandy Bottom's median household income was $8,800 per year; 45 percent of all households had annual incomes of less than $7,500. Sandy Bottom was like many low-income neighborhoods throughout the United States—overwhelmed by internal and external circumstances that held the residents down. Sandy Bottom faced nearly all the problems that a neighborhood can face — from drugs to economic decline, from poverty

One of many extremely dilapidated shotgun houses surrounded by overgrown and trash-filled lots in the six-block area around Bethel AME. In the fall of 1992, these images began to be replaced by neatly landscaped lawns and new single-family homes.

to youth in trouble, from unemployment to absentee landlords.

The community fabric was in shreds, torn by landowners' neglect, lack of adequate social and public services, and the indifference of people who passed through the neighborhood. Years of abandonment, betrayal, and broken promises had made residents very suspicious of outsiders, and unfortunately, that included church folk! There was little trust even among neighbors in Ensley. "About the only time you saw any cooperation was when people got together to go to the shot houses," recalled Ms. Central Jones, a longtime resident of Sandy Bottom. "I knew a few folks, but you really couldn't call it much of a neighborhood anymore."

It is not surprising that residents felt that they had hit bottom, and that the "bottom" was the best they could hope for. To build anything new seemed like building on sand. The name "Sandy Bottom" fit all too well.

## This Is Church Business

It seemed impossible that Sandy Bottom could be rehabilitated. In my first years as pastor, I didn't think that Bethel could to do much more than we were already doing: providing emergency assistance, buying Christmas presents for children and offering free hot meals to the "needy." The needs were too overwhelming. We didn't have the experience nor the resources needed to change Sandy Bottom.

I had to face the reality that Bethel AME is a relatively small church with limited resources. When I was assigned to pastor the church in the late 1980s, fewer than a hundred people attended church on most Sunday mornings. The church itself was in dire need of physical and spiritual revitalization. The basement floor flooded when it rained. The roof leaked. The windows were cracked. Morale was low. And the congregation was having to adjust to its new twenty-seven-year-old pastor fresh out of seminary! Some members argued that we should spend our time tending to "church business" and let "those people" in Sandy Bottom fend for themselves.

But gradually, after talking with Ms. Patton and other residents, I knew that the needs of Sandy Bottom were in fact "church business."

I had seen communities like Sandy Bottom all of my life. In fact, I grew up in very similar conditions. No one ever tried to rehabilitate our neighborhood. In due time, anyone who was able to move away did just that. Streets that had once been our playground became deserted. Our homes were eventually demolished and our neighborhood that had once been full of life and joy became one of the city's many troubled spots.

I was almost convinced that neighborhoods like Sandy Bottom were beyond redemption. They had no choice but to die. It took talking to Ms. Patton and other residents on their front porches to drastically change my opinion and subsequently the course of my life.

AS AN ORGANIZER for Greater Birmingham Ministries, I had worked on social justice issues such as affordable housing, welfare and tax reform. But nothing had ever ignited my passion nor disturbed my spirit quite like the plight of the residents in Sandy Bottom.

After two years of serving as Bethel's pastor, it became more and more difficult for me to pray and preach sermons — sermons about a God who sent His messengers and Messiah out into the world to preach good news to the poor, to clothe, to feed, to bring hope and salvation, to set the prisoners free, and to rebuild ruined places — when all around our very own church were people who were ill-clothed, hungry, full of despair, and living in third-world conditions. Bethel could not be true to the gospel message we preached, nor the faith we claimed to possess, if we failed to act out our faith in practical and relevant ways. Our neighbors in Sandy Bottom deserved more from the church than kind words, superficial relationships, and empty promises. They needed decent affordable housing, adequate health care, a safe environment for children to play and seniors to live, and jobs with decent wages and benefits.

We began to hear God speaking to us through the suffering of this abandoned community. God spoke to us through the desperate need we saw all around us. God challenged us to step outside the doors of our church and to look past our preoccupation with survival and success. It became our calling to embrace our neighbors who lived in crumbling homes all around the church, and to bring tangible signs of hope in a neighborhood filled with despair.

I stopped seeing rundown houses and started seeing "real people." I began to realize that God was speaking through the negative conditions in the community, saying very simply that "something needs to be done in Sandy Bottom to improve the lives of these, 'the least of my children.'"

Should we be surprised that God would speak to us in such a situation? Wouldn't it be even more surprising if God did not speak through the negative images and deplorable conditions that surround our churches?

We decided at Bethel AME, as a community of faith, that it was time to heal the tragic split between the lives of our neighbors and the life of the church. It was time to remember that God became human and dwelt among us to teach us that, even as the sparrows matter to God, how much more precious are human lives and neighborhoods and, indeed, whole cities. We realized that the negatives in Sandy Bottom were actually opportunities for God to "reweave the fabric" of community. The deplorable situation around us became an invitation for all of us to live the gospel itself.

God was calling us to a new mission. And that mission was to demonstrate to the residents of Sandy Bottom that God had not abandoned them, and to create a process to revive, reclaim, and rebuild — not only the community, but individual lives as well.

## God is at work!

The belief that God is at work has been crucial to the work of our church in Ensley. Without this conviction, we might have become imprisoned in hopelessness and stereotyping, with our hearts and minds closed to what we perceived as the will of God for our lives. The constant reminder that "God is at work" has inspired and sustained us despite what often seemed like insurmountable obstacles.

Like Bethel AME, most congregations and neighborhoods are not skilled in many forms of social ministry. However, every congregation can and must engage in ministry that responds not just to its own preferences and survival issues but to the needs of the people within the community — in ways that demonstrate a belief that God is at work.

Unfortunately, instead of encouraging and engaging parishioners to become more involved in troubled neighborhoods, "moving to a more

BEAT was founded in the basement of Bethel African Methodist Episcopal Church in the Ensley community of Birmingham. The church remains the center of the BEAT initiatives.

desirable neighborhood" is high on the wish list for many pastors and congregations. The great lesson of BEAT is that there are sacred places — and opportunities to grow, prosper, and make a difference — right outside our doors.

## Faith makes the difference

While faith is the essential and defining quality of communities we call churches, few pastors and church members believe that they can effect positive change in distraught and despairing neighborhoods. Many churches totally ignore communities in trouble, saying: "we don't have anything to offer"; "it'll take someone with more than what we've got to change that situation"; or "there are more important issues in the church than trying to help those folk who don't care about their own future."

What will inspire the average congregation to abandon excuses such as "we don't know what to do," or "why us," or, especially, the seven last words of many churches, "we've never done it that way before"? During the past decade at Bethel AME, we have learned that for a church to make a difference in a neighborhood and reveal the power of God for new life, it takes only one thing: it takes eyes to see that the very needs of the community are also resources for doing God's work, to see that it takes faith that God can work with what is visible to create great things that are not yet visible.

The Church has a choice to make.

We can either be swept down into the pattern of abandonment that has devastated many African-American communities, or we can stay in our neighborhoods and bring genuine hope anchored in the gospel that the church seeks to proclaim. Ministry requires relationships, trust, and partnerships, but even more profoundly, ministry requires faith. Our faith in God has inspired our vision and hope, and has challenged us to bridge the gap between church and community. God's creative and reconciling power has brought us to the point where residents, merchants, schools, social service agencies, and governments work harmoniously on a common agenda.

## Starting At The Bottom

Attempting to "reweave the fabric" of Sandy Bottom appeared to be an impossible task. Bethel AME Church is by no means a "mega" church. In fact, in 1990 Bethel had an active membership of fewer than one hundred.

A community park was identified by new home owners as one of the vital needs of the neighborhood. The park, named in honor of Bishop C.E. Thomas, a former pastor of Bethel AME, has since been completed. But even the erection of the sign in the photo above was a key symbol of our vision in the early phases of BEAT.

Although the church is fifteen minutes from downtown Birmingham, it is not on a major thoroughfare. In fact, it was on a dead-end street in an isolated community with a very negative image.

Yet, we felt God was calling us to rebuild a six-block area surrounding the church, calling on us to imagine the transformation that could be wrought by constructing seventy-five new homes, improving the infra-structure, creating jobs, and building a community center, neighborhood park, and other amenities. Equally as important, we felt that we were being called to reweave the fabric of community by building trust and caring relationships. Over time, with this vision in our hearts, we had great ideas, good intentions, and an extraordinary sense of determination.

We also had many barriers to overcome:
- Bad Location — The church was not on a major thoroughfare.
- Small Church — Bethel had fewer than one hundred active members.
- Community with a Negative Image — Ensley had acquired a reputa-

In the summer of 1994, BEAT began closing the streets in Sandy Bottom in preparation for the first phase of infrastructure improvement — valued at over a half-million dollars! This was a concrete testimony to the power of our strength as a community working together.

tion as a crime-ridden, drug-infested neighborhood.

- No Money — Preliminary estimates indicated that it would take eight to ten million dollars to redevelop the six-block area surrounding the church. We had absolutely no money in our coffers for such a development.
- No Land — Our goal was to rebuild the community, constructing a minimum of seventy-five new homes. We did not own a single lot in the entire six-block redevelopment area.
- No Expertise in Construction — The initial core group of church members and residents had no experience in building a house, much less redeveloping an entire neighborhood.
- No Credibility in the Broader Philanthropic Community — We were the "new kids on the block" in the nonprofit arena in Birmingham. Consequently, no one with money knew who we were or what we were capable of doing. Because we had no prior relationships with funding agencies, we did not know where to go or how to ap-

proach potential contributors.

- No Track Record — While our initial core group had a variety of different experiences, housing, community development, and community organizing were not among them.

- Not Everyone In the Church Embraced the Vision — There was widespread support within the church for our new community initiative, but a few members of the congregation were vehemently opposed to the effort and argued that our time and efforts would be better spent focusing on the church's success and survival as an institution.

- Lack of Trust — Initially, many of the residents living around the

98-year-old Clara Hall steps out her front door to observe the long-awaited improvements being made to her neighborhood of forty years. Ms. Hall passed away after living in her new duplex home for one week.

church were apprehensive when we started talking about rebuilding the community. There had been a huge gap between the church and the community. Many questioned our motives and were wary about what our actions might mean for their future. They had many concerns: "What is going to happen to me? Will my family be dislocated? Will we have to pay higher rent? How will your plans affect my benefits?"

## The Fruits of Our Labor

Despite the many limitations, obstacles, and questions, we never gave up on our hopes and dreams for a revitalized Sandy Bottom community. Our relentless faith and determination have empowered us to defy the odds and make tangible differences in the community. By not giving up, we were able to accomplish the following:

☐ HOUSING AND COMMUNITY DEVELOPMENT
- Quality, affordable single-family and duplex homes constructed for low and moderate income families.
- Several existing homes renovated.
- Six blocks of property acquired and new infrastructure installed, including lighting, sidewalks, curbs, gutters, underground utilities, and improved sewer and drainage systems.
- Development of a new community center and neighborhood park.

☐ COMMUNITY ORGANIZING AND LEADERSHIP
- New community-owned and -operated businesses in Historic Downtown Ensley, including a family restaurant, a wedding consultant business, a child care center, a welfare-to-work center for single-mothers, and a Jazz School for middle and high school students.
- Acquisition of nearly two blocks of commercial property in Historic Downtown Ensley.
- Street improvements, lighting, and landscaping in the Ensley business district.
- Technical assistance provided to neighborhood businesses
- Revolving loan fund and community emergency fund created

New single-family and duplex homes along Avenue "D" in the Sandy Vista community of Ensley. Prior to BEAT's redevelopment, there were no sidewalks, streetlights, or curbs.

One of the many new 1300-square feet single-family homes in the Sandy Vista community today.

- School-to-Work program which provides employment and training opportunity for high school youth.

☐ YOUTH
- Ensley Youth Council created to equip middle and high school students with leadership skills.
- Tutoring program for more than one hundred children, from ages six to sixteen. Staffed by four churches.

- College Scholarship and Endowment fund for Ensley youth.
- Mentoring program created in collaboration with local churches.
- Summer youth employment program.
- Annual Parent/Youth conference established, offering workshops on conflict resolution, careers, leadership, parenting, and personal development for more than one hundred residents.
- Summer camp that provides educational, recreational, cultural and spiritual enrichment for more than one hundred children, ages six to sixteen.
- Boy Scout and Girls Club organized in the Sandy Vista neighborhood.

☐ FUND RAISING
- Several million dollars raised from public and private sources; churches; civic and neighborhood groups; corporations and banks; local, regional, and national foundations; local, state and federal governments; and individuals.

Eleven-year-old Felicia Fields, and two masked friends, during a break in BEAT summer camp. Our youth activities are an important part of building community togetherness.

# 2

# Getting Started:
# Creating Power by Coming Together

HOW COULD a small church, with limited resources, in a poverty-stricken neighborhood, overcome such formidable barriers to transform the life of a community?

We had made a commitment, but there was no road map for this journey. In the beginning, I didn't know what to do other than to demonstrate in a very personal and honest way that I cared. And that the church cared! Our first major challenge was to restore the hope, trust and compassion that had been crushed by years of abandonment, betrayal, unkept promises, and racial hostility. Nothing meaningful could possibly happen in Sandy Bottom without the reweaving of the fabric of relationships and bridging the huge gap between the church and community.

A crucial first step was forming a core group of people committed to a vision of a revitalized neighborhood. This group would grow into BEAT, the Bethel-Ensley Action Task, Inc. Our initial group was very small, consisting of a few members of the local church, neighborhood residents, and members of Greater Birmingham Ministries. The core group's first task was to organize itself in ways that allowed for accountability, leadership, and planning without jumping ahead to leave the neighborhood itself out.

The core group learned some important lessons along the way.

## 1. Spend time in the community.

It was the responsibility of members of the core group, particularly those who were members of the church, to reconnect with the community. We wanted to meet people where they were and take them seriously as human beings of dignity and potential. Despite the desperate appearance of the neighborhood, we believed that the people had something to offer. We knew we needed to go out into the community instead of asking the community to come to us. Presenting a nonthreatening physical presence in the community became critical. This involved taking time to walk the streets, to listen to what people had to say, to laugh, to talk, to grieve, to accept and respect people regardless of how they looked or sounded, where they lived, or their level of education or economic status. We wanted to convey to our neighbors our conviction that, in the eyes of God, we are all equal, we all make mistakes, and we all have problems, limitations, and weaknesses.

Our outreach effort was not intended to invite, inform, advise, create, or impose an agenda or lifestyle on the community. We simply wanted our neighbors to know that we genuinely cared about them.

## 2. Focus on building relationships.

Relationships are at the heart of the BEAT process. BEAT is not first and foremost about launching a project or building a house. It is about building relationships among people so that isolation ends and trust begins. Building strong healthy relationships is necessary to sustain enduring change. New streets and new homes are just expressions of the change that has already happened. At some point long before the first foundation was poured, the people in the neighborhood realized things were not the same because they were already living together and being together in a new way. Relationships are the key — they make everything else possible.

## 3. Involve the residents.

Involving residents in decision-making and agenda-setting has been the cornerstone of the BEAT process. It is the only way to rebuild the essential element of trust. We believed that everyone had something to bring to the table. In fact, if positive change was to occur in the community, residents had to be at the forefront. It was not enough for members of the church, social service providers, government representatives, or anyone else to articulate and define what was needed in Sandy Bottom. Only the residents could do that. Consequently, before we formulated a mission statement or made the first plans for the organization, it was necessary for the community to be around the table and to inform the process.

## 4. Be willing to give up something!

Engaging the community and establishing new relationships meant we had to give up something. We had to abandon our presumptions, resentments, and pride. We had to abandon indifference and start caring again, caring less about ourselves and more about our neighbors.

Many of us had driven in and out of Ensley for years as if untouched by the conditions and people in the community. Those who had anything to say at all would hang their heads in disgust and recall how the neighborhood once was better and how terrible it had become. "It's just a shame," we would say.

However, when we began associating real faces, stories, and feelings with the visible conditions that Sandy Bottom residents faced day in and day out, the "reality became real" to us for the first time. People in the neighborhood slowly became our neighbors, with names we knew and suffering we could feel. The community's condition became more and more disturbing, but now we also had the passion to try to make life better.

## 5. Let the community set the agenda

One of the very real things that we learned from Sandy Bottom residents was that people felt hopeless. They had been abused, neglected, and devalued for so long that the prospect of change was inconceivable to many.

The Rev. Deborah Grant of Atlanta, Georgia, leading one of the many BEAT-sponsored youth retreats and workshops in the Ensley community.

In practice, this meant that they were equally convinced that their opinions did not matter. No one had ever taken seriously what they had to say. When they talked, nothing seemed to happen because the decisions that affected their lives were usually made without their knowledge, much less their participation. They did not own or control the neighborhood in which they lived, not its land, its businesses, its decision-making processes, nor its future. We wanted the people in the community to know that they did matter and that what they had to say was critical in shaping a community vision and agenda.

## 6. The people are more important than a project!

It was tempting to rush ahead to implement a first project. Implementing a project is easier than the process of building a shared vision. And we were all eager to see some change. We needed something tangible to show to people who said, "I'll believe it when I see it." We could have immediately become consumed with the demands of finding a contractor and designing a house and raising money. But that would have been a big mistake.

Revitalizing a community requires concentrated attention to building relationships and providing opportunities for people to share what is important to them. It is tempting to focus exclusively on some neighborhood project. Projects indeed have a place, but they can also distract from the foundational work of building the table of dialogue, sharing, and visioning. Without a widely agreed upon vision of the church and neighborhood, projects have little impact. Within the context of a broader vision, however, specific projects chosen as priorities by the community have a long-lasting, powerful impact. Community involvement makes the difference. We had to maintain a delicate balance between "making something happen" and building a community vision.

# 3

# The Next Steps

ONCE WE had studied and prayed and prayed and studied some more, we began to feel comfortable with the level of community involvement and support for taking action in Sandy Bottom. However, there were many, many potential projects that could be undertaken. Some were more realistic than others, some more pressing than others. We had to identify which projects had the greatest importance and which ones we were most capable of addressing. Thus, we went through an intensive process of needs assessment, data collection and reporting, strategizing and prioritizing, and development of the organizational tools which would make our dreams become real.

## Assess the needs

Conducting a survey was one technique we used to determine community needs. The survey was a key element in the process of reclamation and community building. It was more than a tool for collecting data; it was a conversation.

The survey took our conversations as a community to another level of interest and involvement. It involved the community in the process of identifying needs, making assessments, organizing strategic planning, and setting priorities.

Although we had laid the groundwork for trust and respect by establishing an open and caring presence in the community for several months, it was important to administer the survey with great sensitivity. Members of the church, residents, former residents, trusted service providers, and local leaders were trained to carry out the survey.

## Report the findings! Report the findings!

Not only did we collect the data, but we were careful to report the findings back to our neighbors after the results were tabulated. Reporting the findings was critical. In many of our communities, "experts" come in frequently to gather data, but people in the neighborhood are rarely privy to the findings or to decisions made based upon the findings. This has made many people in our neighborhoods very uneasy with "surveys" and "studies." Convening community meetings to report the findings was a necessary part of reinventing community. People were able to hear their own voices and those of their neighbors. It was proof that someone was listening and expected to hear them speak again about what would happen next. In fact, community meetings to report the findings evolved into community meetings to identify priorities and decide what would happen next.

## Setting priorities, goals, and guiding principles

When results of the survey were analyzed, decent, affordable housing emerged as the top priority. We held several community meetings to go over survey findings, identify priorities, and articulate our guiding principles.

One of the most empowering aspects of this process occurred when people in the church and neighborhood began making decisions about what could or should be changed and what was important to them. Agreement on these issues led to defining guiding principles and goals. Core group members formulated five goals or principles that would guide future decisions. The principles focused on (1) the central role of the church, (2) inclusiveness, (3) safety, (4) children, and (5) building community.

It took about three months of weekly meetings to determine our guiding principles and values. While this process was often frustrating, it became clear that our labors had laid the foundation for rebuilding community. The process of sharing enable d us to understand what was important to everyone in the group. Everything that subsequently happened in our neighborhood, which was renamed "Sandy Vista" during the process, somehow reflects the goals and principles we established in those early meetings. Moreover, whatever happens in years to come will be a direct result of the guiding principles. Although this early labor required patience and a willingness to be vulnerable and open with other people, today we can see clearly that it made the critical difference in BEAT's eventual success.

Collectively, the guiding principles constitute the measuring rod for the organization and the community. Every decision that the community makes is evaluated in terms of the common values reflected in the principles.

## A name and a mission statement.

After cultivating constructive relationships between the church and the neighborhood and identifying priorities and guiding principles, it was time to formulate a mission statement for revitalizing the neighborhood. We had to decide not only what we would do, but how we would do it.

Our name became Bethel Ensley Action Task, or BEAT. Each word was important. It named the church, the neighborhood, and what we were intent on doing together. We were going to translate the community's hopes into action. We were committed to following through to completion.

BEAT's values and mandates continue to inform its mission. The organization's values incorporate its beliefs; its mandates inform its duties; and its mission reflects its reason for being. Our mission encompassed five primary commitments:

Rev. Nored, right, and Clarence L. Brown, a trustee of Bethel AME and BEAT's first board president, sharing one of their many conversations following a community meeting at Bethel.

1. BEAT will be a self-directing, neighborhood-based organization that is truly representative of the Sandy Bottom community, now renamed Sandy Vista.

2. BEAT will build new homes and rehabilitate existing substandard homes for low-income families in the community.

3. BEAT will facilitate active participation in the revitalization program by a broad cross-section of churches, professionals, governments, businesses, community residents and volunteers from throughout the greater Birmingham area.

4. BEAT will empower the new Sandy Vista area to become a viable, self-directing community with a revitalized social and economic fabric.

5. BEAT will be a responsible custodian of resources entrusted to the organization on behalf of the community and will follow all laws, regulations, and rules that may apply to its operations and organization.

## Forming a nonprofit organization.

In order to allow for broader participation and to meet specific requirements of various funding institutions, we formed a not-for-profit organization called Bethel-Ensley Action Task, Inc. (BEAT, Inc.) as a separate legal entity from the church. The core group of members of the church and community were involved in the process which developed bylaws and articles of incorporation, identified an attorney to file for 501(c) (3) nonprofit designation, and selected a board of directors and an advisory council.

## Looking at other models.

Before finally incorporating and approving the bylaws, we made site visits and met with others who had formed community-based organizations with a commitment to resident involvement.

# 4

# Leadership: Building and Sustaining Commitment to Community Vision

NOTHING IS more important than the right kind of leadership! Community revitalization depends on an empowering leadership — leadership that grows, equips, and encourages the innate leadership abilities of other people. The best leader inspires other people who haven't had the chance to express their God-given gifts and abilities. No leader can substitute for an organized, committed community with a vision.

If control and domination are mistaken for leadership, progress will be short-lived. A "gatekeeper" kind of leader can get in the way, undermine empowerment of the community and destroy its best efforts. It is a challenge for the group to hold its leaders accountable and to insist on an empowering style of leadership.

Some folk think that the strongest leader is the one who can and does control everything. But really, the strongest leader is the one who is strong enough and secure enough to develop new leaders. Some folk think that the leader is supposed to have all the answers. But really, the best leader is the one who makes sure the right questions are asked, and guides the community in finding the answers. Some folk think the best leader is one who will do all the work. But really, the best leader is the one who brings the community and its partners together to share the work. The strongest leader doesn't have to be in control and take all the credit, but instead takes great joy in watching other folks' talents and abilities grow and flourish.

In short, the leader's job is to build the community's capacity to act. Residents of Sandy Bottom had long been given the message that they were "no-count," "no-body," and "know-nothing." Our leaders created a process so that all along the way the abilities and gifts of each person were appreciated and enhanced.

I remember a young lady in our community, Johnnie Luster. Johnnie Luster is a natural-born leader who had never had the chance to lead. There has been no greater joy than seeing Johnny Luster elevated, recognized and celebrated for her God-given leadership qualities. She has served skillfully as the president of the Residents Association. She is now an aide to an Alabama state senator. She has given great leadership to the board of a statewide organization that lobbies the Alabama Legislature in partnership with the poor.

There has been no greater joy than watching Angela and Wilbert Crochen blossom as leaders in the community. Angela dropped out of school when she was fifteen because she was pregnant and on drugs. Will spent time on the streets and in prison. The Crochens turned their lives around. Now they are parents of five children, homeowners in the Sandy Vista neighborhood, and owners of a wedding shop in the Ensley commercial district. In their free time, they work with neighborhood youth, helping them develop into strong, healthy young men and women.

There has been no greater joy than watching two neighborhood boys become fine young leaders. One has become a preacher and the other has become president of the Ensley Youth Council and a gifted orator. They believe in themselves and they have great hopes for the future! More importantly, even at their young age they understand that leadership is about elevating other people.

To lead is to lift up. To lead is to step back so that others can step forward. To lead is to equip, train and nurture others to become effective leaders.

We believe that every person has something of value to offer to our effort. An important role for leaders has been to help each person find a niche. One person may enjoy strategizing and planning, another may need the hands-on experience of picking up trash or laying hammer to nail. One person may enjoy organizing community events; another may have the gift of public speaking. A musician may raise funds through a community concert; another person may have a special love for youth. One person may have a knack for fund raising; another may be able to set up a system for keeping financial records.

## Leadership does not give up

Leadership not only lifts up but it does not give up. There have been times when I felt like giving up, and there have been times when others advised me to give up. Sometimes it seemed that anybody with good sense would give up!

But something has always kept me going. Sometimes it was the look on the face of a single mother when she learned that she could buy her own house through the BEAT program — something she never believed would happen. Sometimes it was seeing a dilapidated shotgun house being demolished and at the same time, the foundation of a new home being poured. Sometimes it just one of the little children coming into my office simply to give me a hug. And sometimes it was when money had gotten so tight that we couldn't make ends meet, only to receive an unexpected gift from a friend.

For me, this was how God reassured me, "Everything is going to be all right. No matter how rough and tough, desperate and despairing the situation might seem — please, don't give up. And, know that there are sources of strength you can call on when your own strength is lagging."

There were plenty of roadblocks. There were plenty of signs saying, "Give up and go back!" For example, as a new church/neighborhood-based organization, our great vision and passion was not enough to convince funders to support our efforts. Because BEAT had no prior relationships with funding sources (*e.g.*, foundations, governments, corporations), it was very difficult to demonstrate that we were a credible organization that could successfully complete our mission and manage major funds efficiently.

Furthermore, many potential donors indicated that our goal of building sixty-four new homes was too ambitious, especially when we had no land, no money, no experience in building even a single house or in organizing a community. Virtually all of the banks, churches, government agencies, and foundations responded in the same way. They thought it was admirable that we wanted to make a difference in the community, but they were unwilling to contribute financially.

Unfortunately, we needed more than kind words — we needed money!

Of course, we knew that some of the skepticism we encountered was valid. We did not own any land in the community. We did not have experience. We had no real credibility outside the neighborhood. The odds did seem to be against us. We could not offer donors a chance to make a big financial return. But we were persistent! We refused to take "no" for an answer. We refused to give up.

Why? We really had no choice. We were like the low-income people in the community. What choice do they have? They have heard "no" for years, but what choice did that leave them except to hang on and keep going even when many of them became discouraged.

We did not allow disappointment to dampen our faith, passion, and love for the people in Sandy Bottom. We experienced the rejection that Sandy Bottom had faced for years, but we knew in our hearts that "no" was no longer an acceptable answer for this community. God was saying, "Yes!" to this small, isolated neighborhood. That's what kept us going through all the frustration, criticism, and discouragement.

This period of time required BEAT's leaders to hold on and be persistent. It tested our determination to lead the neighborhood as a whole. Our determination to hold together as a community was eventually rewarded. After nearly two years of planning, meeting, and efforts to convince others of the merits of our effort (not to mention quite a few rejections!), BEAT received its first grant — one hundred and fifty dollars from a Ensley women's group! It may seem like a small achievement, but that first one hundred and fifty dollars allowed BEAT to buy an option on a lot where the first house would be built. Beyond that, it meant that the community was beginning to step forward, even though the odds were long and we had nothing tangible to show for two years of work! The community's commitment had not wavered, even though its monetary resources were small.

The gift from the women's group was followed by a significant grant by the board of directors of Greater Birmingham Ministries, an interfaith urban mission agency in Birmingham. With this grant we were able to purchase the property on which we had purchased the option. A local church followed with a donation of twenty-five thousand dollars. Soon afterward, the City of Birmingham granted BEAT over two hundred thousand dollars. In one year, that one hundred and fifty dollars grew to over one million dollars! Our leaders refused to give up, and it paid off in an amazing way!

## Leadership seeks to be trustworthy

Transforming leadership must prove itself to be trustworthy. This means being faithful to the people you are serving. When we started the BEAT program, we met with a lot of distrust from the City, the community, and funders. People always questioned our motives. And perhaps rightly so, because they have been hurt too many times by someone or some group making promises they couldn't deliver. Too many people come into poor communities offering a quick fix, and then leave taking something with them that they have no right to take, leaving the community worse off than it was before they came.

Leadership must be trustworthy. You have to prove that you are worthy of trust. That means acting with integrity and being a good steward of the money that has been entrusted to you. It means doing what you say you are going to do, and being accountable when you fail to do what you said you were going to do. Earning trust, I've learned, sometimes requires showing that you care about the people and the process more than getting your own way.

Perhaps the best way to talk about leadership is to talk about leaders. It has been a source of constant amazement and joy to witness the blossoming leadership of Sandy Bottom residents and Bethel AME church members.

CLARENCE BROWN is a longtime member of Bethel AME Church in the Sandy Bottom neighborhood of Ensley. As an employee of the U.S. Department of Labor and an African-American, Clarence has seen just how hard it can be for one individual to raise himself out of poverty, much less an entire neighborhood. Clarence has served as the president of BEAT from its inception.

> I think BEAT represents for me the crossroads in my life. I have been involved in the community for a long time. Until I started to give my life in trying to revitalize Sandy Bottom, very few times have I actually seen some tangible products result from my actions. BEAT has been sort of reinvigorating and inspiring for me.
>
> I believe that we all have civic rent to pay. Somewhere along the way, someone has made some sacrifice for us. Giving my time and energy to fulfill our dream of improving the quality of life for residents in Ensley has been my way of trying to give something back. What better way to do that than through the church? The church is the resourceful answer to the problems, particularly in our urban communities.
>
> What does BEAT mean for Clarence Brown? It means that I am a volunteer for life. I just believe in people. I believe that each and every one of us has something within us that can make our neighborhoods stronger and healthier. I have always been a person who wanted to see Ensley revitalized. BEAT undoubtedly was the vehicle to do just that.
>
> The fact that there is an active leadership through the neighborhood association demonstrated clearly to me that residents in the community simply wanted an opportunity to channel their thoughts and actions where they, too, could make a difference.

FLORINE HUFF, eighty-two, a longtime resident of Ensley, has been a member of the BEAT board for six years.

> When I heard about the dream of a revitalized Sandy Bottom and saw neighbors coming together, I was determined to do what I could to make sure the vision became a reality. I was president of the Ensley Community Aid Club and along with Birlie Brown, a member of Bethel AME Church. We convinced our small club to make a contribution to BEAT to secure an option on a piece of property that was available for purchase in the redevelopment area. Some people call it the widow's mite that made the difference. All we know is that we were determined to do what we could, big or small.

HENRY SCRUGGS: Henry, a member of Bethel AME, was no stranger to Sandy Bottom in 1990. When BEAT began, he was running a small, one-man construction company in the western area of Birmingham, but he was not directly focused on Sandy Bottom. As BEAT's construction manager, he now has more than thirty new houses to his credit.

I became involved in BEAT early on. Reverend Nored and Clarence Brown had been working on getting the first house built, and they finally had purchased a vacant lot. But they still had no one to build a house that a low-income family could afford.

One day I was coming out of church and Reverend Nored and Clarence approached me again. They told me they needed a contractor and that they wouldn't be able to pay a whole lot. I told them I would help out as much as I could, and then they asked me if I knew other contractors, carpenters, and plumbers who might be willing to help out at little or no cost. I told them that I would ask some of the people who had worked with me on various projects. They all said they would contribute their time.

We started out working in our spare time, after work and on Saturdays. But it was going too slow and all of us could see that. So we all decided that we needed to work on it full-time as much as we could. And after that it speeded up a lot. I wasn't able to do much more than pay their gas money for a long time, and each of us would "go sneaking off" to put on a doorknob here or repair a roof there in order to have enough to live on.

But we just kept on, and that group of small black construction people built that first house, to tell you the truth, and I really don't think it would have happened without them just deciding that they were going to make it happen. And God got us all through it somehow. All that was very important because once we finished the first house, people began to see that something could and would happen.

Since finishing the first house, interestingly enough, we are all still working together. Today I am able to compensate some of those guys who volunteered their time initially. In fact, for myself and some carpenters who worked at BEAT, Sandy Vista has now become a full-time job.

BEAT has also been responsible for growth in the businesses of plumbers, carpenters, electricians and roofers who have volunteered on the job site. It's been good for everybody.

# 5

# Planning: The Key to Success

PLANNING IS the key to success of any church/neighborhood partnership. Proper planning reveals the things that are essential and methodically outlines the steps for accomplishing important tasks. Planning allows for broad-based, community participation — or at least it should. Before we built our first house, initiated any programs, or actively pursued funding sources, members of the church and community, along with architects, engineers, contractors, and other specialists, spent fifteen months thinking through all of the issues involved in rebuilding Sandy Bottom and developing strategies to accomplish our goals. Fifteen months!

Amazingly enough, although it was frustrating and tedious at the time, that period of planning did not slow down the overall process. It actually enabled us to anticipate and address issues that would inevitably arise, perhaps at a more critical juncture in the process. We learned that a group can either spend time at the front end of a process, building trust and involving the community in decision-making, or it will spend even more time later in the process, trying to repair broken relationships or create trust in the middle of a very intense decision-making period.

Similarly, if you move too quickly to implementation, there may be no clear consensus about how decisions are made or who makes them. This can cause the community-based process to start to break down and people to walk away. It can create a tragic amount of conflict that can erode trust that has been so carefully constructed.

Because we spent over a year in planning, when it came time to act, we were equipped to move forward. For the most part, all we had to do was to fill in the blanks of a strategy or procedure that the planning process had anticipated. After we completed one step in the planning process, we simply took the next step. We watched groups which had neglected the planning process be forced later to stop midstream to address issues that should have been resolved earlier. Such delays led to frustration, discouragement, loss of participation, and increased costs.

BEAT's planning process also helped convince potential funders in city government, foundations, and the corporate community that we had carefully thought through the issues associated with every phase of development and that we were serious about our work. It added to our credibility and enhanced funders' trust in the community and its process. Planning helped us see how the barriers we anticipated could be overcome.

## Strategic planning is critical!

The strategic plan we developed over those fifteen months clarified the major issues facing BEAT and suggested ways of resolving those issues. It also served as a model for the ongoing process of strategic thinking. This strategic plan represented a fine-tuning of BEAT as an organization.

Members of Bethel AME Church and residents of Sandy Bottom identified several issues in the early stages of community development. Most of the concerns and issues were still being debated two years after the BEAT program started. At that time, only two new houses were under construction. None had been completed.

BEAT's strategic, community-based planning process began in 1991. It was led by Richard "Dick" Pigford, head of a group of volunteer design professionals called the "Tuesday Group," Rick Ambrose, a BEAT board member, and several students in the masters in public administration program at the University of Alabama. The process identified a number of critical issues facing BEAT.

## The Internal Environment

BEAT's greatest internal resources were the high levels of motivation and diverse talents among Sandy Bottom residents, church members, and volunteers from other communities. Within the organization there was an ample supply of skilled volunteers who possessed a wide range of skills. BEAT board members and volunteers offered technical, professional, trade, skilled and unskilled labor at no charge. Although the BEAT board was not highly experienced as a community development agency, the organization consistently demonstrated a strong presence, process, and strategy.

There were, however, some internal weaknesses in the early stages. BEAT was a young organization with no history of solving major crises on its own. Initially, there was no formal organizational structure. Board members lacked experience in operating a community development corporation, and each group of professionals among BEAT's nonresident members had its own perspective and view of priorities.

## The External Environment

The most positive external forces affecting BEAT's mission were the popularity of "holistic" approaches to neighborhood reclamation and the political and social clout of BEAT's partners. The leadership of the City of Birmingham and several local churches had demonstrated a willingness to provide support for low-income housing development. By supporting BEAT, well-established social agencies such as Greater Birmingham Ministries, Neighborhood Services Incorporated, and the Campaign for Human Development helped to legitimize our mission and our plan. Excellent coverage from the media also helped to increase community support.

Churches, government agencies, social service agencies, and volunteers were strong partners. In addition to lending their reputation to BEAT, they offered direct, concrete support. Several area churches regularly provided funding and volunteer labor. The City of Birmingham provided funding, technical assistance, and political support. Social service agencies like Neighborhood Services and Greater Birmingham Ministries devoted

BEAT architect Richard "Dick" Pigford, far right, in a meeting with representatives of the Associated General Contractors of Birmingham, who provided
more than $100,000 of in-kind services to build a new community center in the
Sandy Vista neighborhood. Dick Pigford has been one of BEAT's strongest
supporters.

resources and staff support, as well as direct counseling services to Sandy
Bottom residents. Volunteer architects provided free community planning and design services.

## Critical Issues

We identified four critical issues that directly influenced BEAT's ability
to achieve its mission:

• **Should BEAT expand the scope of its operations beyond the Sandy
Bottom neighborhood?** While we wanted to help other communities,
BEAT's neighborhood identity was one of its greatest strengths. BEAT's
mission was rooted in the Sandy Bottom community and its residents. We
decided to focus on the Sandy Bottom area, but also to help other organizations replicate BEAT. Expanding BEAT's scope beyond Sandy Bottom
in the early years would have interfered with the successful completion of

our core mission. BEAT has now helped seven other groups emulate its community development process, and this book is a part of our planned outreach. After several years of success, BEAT did expand its scope to include revitalization of the larger Ensley community.

• **How should BEAT allocate resources between the housing rehabilitation and community/social development functions?** BEAT's mission was to facilitate the redevelopment of the entire community—physical, social, and economic. There was a danger in letting house construction become so all consuming that other facets of community development might be neglected (*e.g.,* youth programs, outreach to senior citizens, neighborhood organization, economic development, leadership training, business incubation). Nevertheless, home construction was what BEAT did best and the activity that generated its greatest support. The challenge we faced was achieving the right balance. We decided that BEAT should continue its focus on housing while experimenting with community development programs. We expected that housing development would equip us with the knowledge, experience, and resources for community development projects on an even larger scale. Also, BEAT's success in housing would help secure support for less tangible community development projects. Over time, BEAT has methodically expanded its involvement and its experience in many areas of community development, especially with the launching of the Ensley Community Issues Forum in 1994. This has led to a comprehensive community-based revitalization effort for the entire Ensley area, encompassing six neighborhoods and a major commercial district.

• **Should BEAT hire an executive director, and if so, should that person be part-time or full-time?** As BEAT's level of activity and success increased, it became apparent that an executive director was needed to provide essential organizational leadership. An executive director could help set priorities, focus the board's decision-making activities, and oversee implementation. It was very difficult at times to coordinate our efforts and remain on track because we had no full-time staff and relied so heavily upon volunteers. A grant from the Campaign for Human Development made it possible for BEAT to hire full-time staff. After two years of leading the BEAT efforts as a pastor and GBM staff member, I was hired as

BEAT's Executive Director in 1992. Today BEAT has an executive director, a financial manager, a youth coordinator, an economic development staff person, and a construction manager.

**How can BEAT obtain long-term funding for day-to day operations and for non-capital community development projects?** Grants generally are awarded for a limited time and are more readily available for capital improvements (*e.g.,* buildings and facilities) and short-term projects. Few foundations will fund general operations or administrative expenses. Non-capital projects implicit in BEAT's mission — social services, community development, and economic assistance — depended upon a stable funding base. A stable funding base was needed to sustain the physical improvements in the community, and to address the social and economic problems of the community as well. We did not want to wind up with seventy-five new houses in a neighborhood that could not sustain itself socially or economically.

OVER ITS six-year history, BEAT has received millions of dollars in grants from foundations, corporations, individuals and other entities. We've come a long way from our first one hundred and fifty dollar grant! Our success in raising funds stems from good long-range planning, a solid track record, and a complex network of partnerships that we have built across the city of Birmingham and, indeed, across the country.

A fifth issue involved revisiting BEAT's Mission and Mandates. Our strategic planning process clarified many issues and fine-tuned the original mission set by the community. The strategic plan enabled BEAT to determine how to accomplish what the community wanted and how to preserve the community-driven nature of the organization. Once we finished the strategic plan, community representatives revised our original mandates and mission to make them more specific and to define our values and goals within the context of the community revitalization process.

## Mandates:

- BEAT housing is restricted to low-income families.
- The board must be representative of the church and community.

• No religious affiliation requirement can be placed on residents who benefit from BEAT programs.

• BEAT must comply with legal restrictions for 501(c)(3).

• BEAT must be an Affirmative Action/Equal Opportunity Employer.

• All housing must meet the building code standards and zoning restrictions.

• City-funded operations are restricted to a declared City of Birmingham urban revitalization district.

## BEAT'S Mission:

Revitalize the Sandy Bottom community through a commitment to:

• Be a self-directing church/neighborhood-based organization that is representative of the Sandy Bottom community.

• Build new homes and rehabilitate existing substandard homes for low and very low income families in Sandy Bottom.

• Facilitate the active participation in the revitalization program of a broad cross-section of churches, professionals, governments, businesses, and individuals volunteers from throughout the Greater Birmingham area.

• Empower the Sandy Bottom community to become a viable, self-directed community with a viable social and economic fabric.

• Be a responsible custodian of the resources entrusted to BEAT on behalf of the community.

This mission statement has guided BEAT's plans and actions since completion of the strategic planning process.

# 5

# What the Larger Community Can Do

TROUBLED neighborhoods like Sandy Bottom have been neglected and abandoned by the larger community. They are cut off socially, physically, and economically from the rest of the community. BEAT's efforts within the Sandy Bottom neighborhood were crucial to rebuilding the internal life of the community, which in turn opened the way for reconnecting with churches, businesses, lenders, colleges, civic and other organizations throughout the city.

We knew that we had to take control of the destiny of our community. But at the same time, we knew that we couldn't do it all by ourselves. The community was rich in its own internal resources, but we still needed resources from the broader community.

## The Power of Partnerships

Building relationships among community members and with outside partners has been the secret to our success. Nothing is more important than relationships! Since our work began, we have aggressively sought a wide range of partners to assist in the development of the Ensley community. We have made hundreds of presentations at churches, synagogues, civic clubs, business organizations, neighborhood groups — we went any-where that we could find an open door and an open ear. We had crafted a vision that was large enough to be shared by everyone. We welcomed each and every person we met to our table. And we could always find some-thing meaningful and productive for each person to do.

We have learned that hope is a irresistible thing. People are drawn toward hope. When they see an effort like BEAT, where hope for change is rewarded, they are eager to give a part of themselves.

The relationships that BEAT nurtured within the community itself and with a few people outside the neighborhood grew step-by-step into a complex network of partnerships. For example, board members from Greater Birmingham Ministries (GBM) began to speak to their own con-gregations, and friends spoke to friends in congregations, businesses, civic groups, and governmental offices. Following GBM's early contribution which allowed BEAT to buy its first lot, Independent Presbyterian Church in Birmingham became our initial construction partner, commit-ting volunteers and financing to build the first house. The *Birmingham Post-Herald,* a local newspaper, committed a year's coverage to our com-munity-based effort and invited others to participate.

Growing support from Mayor Richard Arrington, Birmingham's City Council members, and Birmingham city department leaders helped move us toward our goal. BEAT began to access local and federal dollars to keep the process going.

Since 1992, more than a hundred different groups representing churches, governments, schools, design professionals, corporations, civic groups, social services agencies, and foundations have become partners with BEAT. These partners invested their time and resources in BEAT because they could see that it would pay off in many ways. They could see some things that they needed to see:

• BEAT offered a win-win situation from which each partner would benefit.

　• Our local group was well organized.

　• Our local group had invested time and resources.

　• Vision and needs were clearly defined and well-articulated.

　• We had an accountable financial system.

- We had nonprofit 501(c)(3) IRS tax status.
- The project had potential for replication.
- There were measurable outcomes.
- The focus was on capacity building for residents.
- People in the community of need were directly involved and on the policy-making board.
- The project was manageable; there is a broad vision but also achievable short-term goals.
- The project has broad implications.
- Other groups were funding the project.
- Grant proposals were well written.
- Projects were completed in a timely fashion.
- We had a positive track record.
- The effort was collaborative, with participation from a diverse set of groups and individuals, including technical experts.
- There was broad-based participation.
- The overall plan included the goal of long-term self-sufficiency.
- There were short- and long-term goals.
- The program was innovative.
- The group's leadership had the trust of the local and broader community.

IN THE remaining portion of this chapter, individuals and representatives from various partner groups who have been involved in the BEAT program share their experiences and their impressions. These statements are offered for three primary reasons. First, they provide insight into motivation — what makes people and institutions become involved in community development efforts. Second, they supplement earlier accounts of the sequence of events leading to BEAT's success, providing the perspectives of partners and workers. Finally, these statements illustrate that successful collaboration creates a win-win situation for those involved.

**MIKE HARPER** was president of the board of directors of Greater Birmingham Ministries (GBM) when BEAT was just beginning. In 1990, GBM's board of directors approved one of the first major financial commitments to BEAT. Mike was also the pastor of the Vestavia Hills United Methodist Church in an affluent, "over the mountain" southern suburb of metropolitan Birmingham. Through the BEAT project, Mike and Vestavia Hills began a cooperative partnership that has linked this predominantly white, upper-income community to the predominantly low-income African American neighborhood of Sandy Bottom. It is a friend-ship and relationship that has continued to this day.

My earliest recollection of the BEAT project is my memory of serving as president of the board of GBM when we made a major decision to give seventy-five thousand dollars from some unused Community Develop-ment Block Grant money to an idea that had been brewing in Ron, Clarence, and other members of Bethel AME. Ron was the economic justice organizer for Greater Birmingham Ministries and pastor of Bethel AME at the time.

I'll never forget the deep sense of pride I had in being able to "jump start" the project. I also remember the wonderful partnership that devel-oped between Vestavia Hills United Methodist Church and Bethel AME Church as the project matured. My most vivid memory of those days was a Saturday when approximately forty persons from our congregation as-sisted members of the church and community in clearing several lots around the church for future development. I also remember the commit-ted labor of several of our retired men and others in construction on some of the first few houses.

It was clear to me that we were both building homes and community. We came to know each other, to trust each other, to laugh and to cry and to eat together. And we learned from each other. We learned the lessons of community and cooperation. We learned that we need each other to make our communities whole. The BEAT project has blossomed into a major investment in Ensley and stands today as a superior example of what can be accomplished with great dreams, hard work, and a collabora-tive and cooperative spirit.

The profound and continuing effect this involvement has had on a white, middle class, "over the mountain" congregation has been one of the more helpful ways to stimulate growth and interaction among races, socioeconomic groups.

**DICK PIGFORD** is founder of the "Tuesday Group," a nonprofit organization of architects, engineers, planners and other professionals who volunteer their service to neighborhoods in need. Dick has been working with BEAT since 1991. The Tuesday Group works in partnership with local citizens and grass-roots organizations. Members of the nonprofit organization help groups analyze their community's problems, set realistic goals, understand specific issues, develop effective strategies, mobilize resources, and design houses.

For me, my participation in Sandy Bottom is a question of Christian stewardship, and I guess in defining stewardship, it is the raising of people, not just the raising of money. And I believe that these are some gifts that I have been given in being an architect, helping people ask questions and decide how people and neighborhoods will use places that will be built. And you have to do that with people. In Birmingham, without the Tuesday Group and the architects involved in it, there would be few if any ways for a neighborhood to find the kind of help they need in making these decisions with all the information that they really need.

There are people out there willing to help and there are neighborhoods looking for this kind of partnership with professionals. In my case, it was a single individual, namely Ron, but there needs to be a mechanism for bringing people together. There are advantages with an individual being that mechanism, but be it networks or organizations, someone has to bring people together face-to-face. Successful work is finally an expression of trust. And that trust has to be built between everyone involved.

Someone from inside the neighborhood has to build trust among a group of people inside the neighborhood, and then the trust has to be built between that group and others in the broader community. That's the role of leadership. Leadership is about trust-building among people, not controlling people or making their decisions for them.

How do you convince people, and yourself, that what you are doing is the right thing? I think it is human nature to question any new idea, especially ones that are difficult or seem impossible on the surface. Building trust is what makes all the difference.

All the things that might have been difficult or challenges to my working with the community were resolved by how the leadership of the neighborhood and of the church brought me into the community. How a person comes into a community is very important. I think that the aspect of being a listener is very important. That's the challenge for a person in a new setting—to be a listener first.

The biggest challenge for me is just finding the hours in the day. I haven't faced any real challenges in relating to the community. There have been some disappointments from a personal point of view in trying to work in other communities, where the issue of undeveloped trust has arisen. And that is a real challenge. It's probably a matter of time. It cannot happen overnight. That isn't real trust. After there is enough experience of a person, then trust is possible because it is an issue of relationship.

Relationships are what the BEAT process is all about. It is not first and foremost doing a project or building a house. It is about building relationships among people so that the isolation ends and the trust begins. That's when it goes beyond partnership. Partners are important. They come in and play a very essential role. But relationships go deeper. They are seen in the people who come in and don't go away. They may not live there, but their hearts are there, and they come back again and again.

The excitement for me is when people realize that what they are doing is change. It doesn't really require that a new street be built. But there is some point in there where the people involved realize that this place is now different. The new or deepened relationships among the people is what makes for change. The new streets or the new houses are just the expression of the change that has already happened. At some point or some day, they realize it is a different neighborhood because they have experienced a different way of living together and being together. And that is really what this is all about.

**LARRY WATTS** is a United Methodist church member and also an experienced community planner. He has assisted with various aspects of BEAT and has just helped the entire Ensley community complete a comprehensive plan for economic and social revitalization of the larger

Ensley community of which Sandy Bottom is a part. BEAT initiated the community-wide revitalization process using the lessons learned in Sandy Bottom. Larry has recently become Director of the Birmingham Regional Planning Commission for metropolitan Birmingham.

Let me tell you just a little bit about my involvement with BEAT. I worked on about three houses out here. I was impressed with the commitment of the people in BEAT, to the point that I rejoined a board that I was on, the board of Greater Birmingham Ministries. My ulterior motive in rejoining was that GBM had an association with Ron Nored and BEAT, and I wanted to see how we could take the BEAT model and apply it somewhere else. That was my secret reason for making the connection with BEAT for what I hoped we could do in Ensley but also well beyond this community.

This was in most ways a unique planning approach based on reality and economic vitality that flowed out of a commitment from the city and the community to do real live community development in an area that is struggling, with limited resources. In much of planning, historically, there has been a tendency to go in and do a project or two and then walk away and feel good that you have done something and go on to the next one; this plan is about fundamental structure and change and creating something that can sustain itself.

We were after some sort of fundamental structure that is not just a drawing, but a living plan that is an expression of the community's own thoughts and direction. Take the BEAT concept that takes a small piece of territory, empowering people in that local territory with resources, see what they can do, then having control over that territory. That's what is crucial to replicate about BEAT. It is the only way community redevelopment will work. We certainly cannot rely on one or two projects for an area. There has to be some activation of the people themselves and find the potential of the people and the potential of the area.

**SUSAN ATKINSON,** planning assistant:

One of the other things that Ensley has lost is community-based services and industry. That's one of the most exciting things to contemplate as an opportunity from here on. There is the large-scale component of

Building and strengthening the capacity of youth in the Ensley community has been one of BEAT's primary goals. At left, children participating in BEAT's annual summer camp at Bethel AME. Over 100 low-income children attend this camp every year. For many, it is their opportunity to go to a camp. In addition to educational and recreational programs, the participants also volunteer at local homeless shelters for women and children, Greater Birmingham Ministries, an urban mission agency, and the Positive Maturity Senior Citizens Center in Ensley.

economic revitalization involving the USX property. But there is a lot of potential in the area of rebuilding community-based services and businesses that are owned and operated by and for people in the area. There are some family-owned businesses that still exist here, and I think the very closeness of those stores to the community makes them stay and quite profitable.

Construction trades also represent the obvious connection to community revitalization, both in building homes and in revitalizing the economic and commercial areas.

**BOB DICKERSON** is an experienced banker in Birmingham with a long history of trying to find ways to bring investment and economic revitalization into low-income neighborhoods.

I got involved with BEAT all the way back when I was working for a local bank and came over here to meet with them. I think there might have been two houses up at that point. I became aware of the organization and really got here through Clarence Brown. I left banking in 1984 and took a city contract to do consulting on community development. One of the theories that I brought to BEAT and other neighborhoods as a former CRA (Community Reinvestment Act) officer was that to make the CRA more effective, more work needed to be done within community organizations themselves. The more results that the banks see, it brings more involvement from the entire financial network of an area.

**STEVE THOMAS** is an officer with Collateral Mortgage, a local financial institution that has been a major partner with BEAT in many ways, including providing financing for potential homeowners in Ensley.

In doing financing, it was important for us to come out and meet Ron, find out his background, and what some of his goals and objectives were. The first thing I remember is thinking that I cannot believe this guy wants to do this in Ensley. But he did. He had a tremendous commitment to it, and it was really in his heart, with such a burning cause. At that time there were three nice looking houses that people were living in with this small project, and the church right there in the center of it, and then a block out it was really discouraging.

So I told Ron right then, "We want to use what resources we have to help you with this project." And he hasn't been bashful about telling us where we could help, and we've tried to be as helpful as we possibly can. It seems like the first thing that I did as an involvement in it was I handled a construction loan for one of the applicants. That turned out to be very, very gratifying. Not too many people at the bank were involved in that, but when we finished the house—we were not involved in the construction of the house, but we handled the construction loan—they invited me to the house blessing ceremony. I was just really gripped when I saw the smile on the lady's face who was going to own the house.

From there we had an opportunity to participate with one of the local churches, St. Mary's Episcopal Church, that is one of our neighbors outside Ensley itself. They wanted to help out with financing two of the houses in BEAT, and they wanted someone to go in as partners with them and handle the other fifty percent of the construction loan basis and they were looking for someone who would actually monitor the construction. We accepted and said we would be happy to do that. So St. Mary's put up some seed money of thirty thousand dollars in an account for two houses, and at that time houses were costing about thirty thousand dollars. So we then came in and arranged the construction loan. And we have just closed out the second of those.

Sometime along in there, Ron said to me, "Wouldn't it be great if New South Federal and Collateral would sponsor a house?" And I said, "Yes, it would. I don't know that we would be able to do it by ourselves, but let me see what we can do." I talked to the president of our bank, Winston Porter, and Winston actually suggested that we see if we couldn't pull together smaller banks like ourselves who would be willing to go together. And we did that. Winston was really instrumental in that, getting the ball rolling by calling folks at banks. We and the other banks formed Banks for Community Housing or BACH. We built the house, and in our organization we had a total of fifty or sixty people involved in building that house, working Tuesday, Thursday and Saturday. Saturday they donated their time. We are very proud of the fact that we built that house in record time and that we were the very first bank group to sponsor a house. And after we did it, several of the larger banks jumped in and built one. I have to feel like we really started something, and we are certainly proud of that.

Then what really hit home to us was that we had a young lady who was an employee of ours, Carolyn Jordan's her name, and there is no way she could have afforded a house, but we introduced her to the BEAT program, she qualified, and she and her family are now living in one of the houses. I see Carolyn every day, and I can tell you that she is certainly grateful for the home.

She's a homeowner. She's paid for the home. She can afford to pay for the home because of the program here. She's involved in a community where there's a community atmosphere. I often wonder where she would be, where she and her family would be living, and what type of environment she would be in if it were not for BEAT. And I know she is very proud of having the home and where it's located.

We have done some other things. We helped arrange some other loans and we have also helped supply funds with some working capital until some of their other donations have come in.

I tell you another interesting story. In the first few months that I was here, I met the construction foreman and supervisor, Henry Scruggs. And I tell you what, he seemed to know a lot about the construction of houses, but he was operating on a very, very small scale. And I have watched him grow over the last few years, that guy has learned more about business and really, truly building houses as the owner of a small business. First of all, he is a very, very hard working individual and very dedicated to his profession. But I don't think Henry Scruggs would have had the opportunity to do nearly what he has done if it had not been for BEAT.

So, those are just a few of the stories we can tell. We as a savings bank remain very interested in this kind of work and using our resources to assist with this kind of community program. We are not a large bank so it is not easy for us to have a large presence in the community, so the BEAT program is an ideal kind of program for us to participate in and know that we can make a difference.

**ROBERT HOLMES** represents Alabama Power, a statewide electric utility company, which has been a financial sponsor of BEAT and has recently awarded BEAT a significant grant from its in-house foundation to help build a community center.

I grew up a mile from here. I now live in Hoover after working for the Power Company. But when I heard that these kinds of things were happening within hollering distance of my old neighborhood, I was excited. This was a neighborhood that I was afraid to come into even as a youth. It was just considered a tough, tough neighborhood. And to see now how it has just completely turned around is just so encouraging. But there was a long tradition here of this being a tough place.

And I think it is particularly encouraging that this is happening in a place like Birmingham that has an image of an old culture that tends to talk a lot without doing a lot and one that is tied to a history of racism, to see this kind of multicultural effort here is just really good. I talk about BEAT all over the country, wherever I am, as an example of what Americans can do if they come together.

I had gotten to know Ron through Leadership Birmingham, and when I learned that there really was no place for young people to gather and to socialize, we, the Power Company, through our foundation, were able to participate in funding the construction of a community center for the youth. It is just essential that young people have that kind of place if they are really going to be a part of a community, and so we were glad to have that opportunity to participate in that way.

# 6

# Broadening the Vision

THE transformation of the six-block Sandy Bottom neighborhood buoyed the hopes and confidence of the entire Ensley community. In time, the neighborhood decided to change its name from Sandy Bottom to Sandy Vista. It was a major statement about just how far this little neighborhood had come.

If new life could happen in a dying place like Sandy Bottom, then it seemed possible that the rest of Ensley could also be transformed. BEAT leaders set their sights on the range of concerns confronting the larger Ensley community. The BEAT process was put to the test: Could it work in a larger geographic area? Could it effectively address issues beyond housing?

The answer is a resounding yes. The BEAT process offers great promise for solving inner-city problems. The BEAT process has been effective — not only in a six-block area, but also in a six-neighborhood region of a city; not only in housing but also economic development and youth development.

After a few years of successful housing work, BEAT expanded its mission to focus on youth and economic development in the larger Ensley community. Several years of work laid the groundwork necessary for an expanded mission. BEAT had built a solid track record. The capacity of the board and staff had been strengthened. Relationships of trust had been built among residents, the mayor and city government, church, schools and corporate leaders; and a team of advisors including architects, lenders, real estate developers, urban planners, and funders.

We knew that in order to address broader community problems, the wider community needed to have ownership from the very beginning. We reached out to the entire Ensley community, an area which includes six neighborhoods and fifteen thousand residents. Churches, businesses, social service agencies, schools, and residents were invited to a series of community meetings. The meetings were held in several different places. They were structured to encourage community members to talk with one another about their vision for Ensley's future.

The meetings brought the community together to build relationships, develop a common vision, and lay the groundwork for collective work. Through these meetings, economic development and youth were lifted up as community priorities. The need for a community-wide organization became apparent. The Ensley Community Issues Forum was formed by BEAT to enable the broader community to address common issues. A fifteen-member board of directors was established with representation from neighborhood associations, churches, social service agencies, businesses, schools, and youth. Economic Development and Youth Committees were created to carry out the work.

## A Shared Vision for Ensley's Future

While youth and economic development were identified as priorities, a comprehensive strategy was still needed. With the support of the city, urban planning consultants were employed to assist the community in launching a long-range planning process. Board members and consultants formed a long-range planning team.

The planning process involved a second series of community meetings. All sectors of the community were invited to participate. Six areas of concern were identified: housing, youth, commercial revitalization, jobs, human services, and design/environment. In each of these areas, community members identified strengths, weaknesses, opportunities, and threats. They identified key issues in each area. Planners compiled information regarding existing conditions, socioeconomic factors, market conditions, and major planning influences.

At each juncture, information was brought back to community meetings for residents' response. This was essential for trust building. We did not want to analyze and use the information in the name of the community without the community's consent. Instead, we brought back to the community the collective voice which emerged from the planning process. The community was then able to craft a shared vision and to organize around it to bring about real change.

A mission statement for the Ensley Forum was adopted:

> The Ensley Community Issues Forum is a grassroots coalition of neighborhoods, churches, schools, agencies, businesses, and residents seeking a life of abundance, security, and community for all Ensley residents.

> The purposes of the Ensley Community Issues Forum are:

> 1) Economic Development: to develop a sustainable local economy with good jobs, viable businesses, and increased community ownership and control;

> 2) Youth Development: to empower youth to be involved in all aspects of community life and leadership;

> 3) Human Services: to improve access to transportation, health care and other human services; and

> 4) Community Organizing: to organize the Ensley community to participate effectively in decisions that affect the community.

## A Long-Range Strategy

The mission statement guides the day-to-day work of the Ensley Forum. The long-range plan laid out a vision for the future of the Ensley community. With a mission statement and vision in place, the Ensley Forum then had to tackle the nitty-gritty work that has steadily produced tangible, visible change.

One important lesson that emerged from BEAT's experience is that community transformation cannot be done piecemeal. Before the first brick is laid, a comprehensive plan must be developed. Planning is critical, but it takes a lot of time and countless meetings. It requires a great deal of patience and persistence. Community people can become frustrated with a prolonged planning process. You may hear people grumbling under their breath, "This is all talk and no action. I thought we were going to do something!" For this reason, it is critical to bring about short-term, visible changes all along the way. A cleanup day, a Christmas tree lighting, a community festival or concert, a dinner to honor community leaders, news coverage about the work—all of these things helped people see that action was indeed happening. These incremental steps have helped to sustain us through the painstaking work of revitalization. Drawings and models have helped people visualize and begin trust that great things that are about to happen.

## Fruits of the Broader Process

The BEAT process works. Its major attributes can be summarized in the principles given below.

    1) The vision emerges from the community.

    2) Planning and implementation is directed by the community.

    3) Attention is given both to tangible, visible change (e.g., building new houses) and to intangible transformation (e.g., enabling residents, building relationships and partnerships).

    4) The process is spiritually grounded.

    5) The community seeks partners who can bring expertise and resources, but who will also accept the community's leadership, honor the community's vision, and accept as well as bring change.

If these principles are honored, this process will work anywhere, on any issue. In Ensley, the process has brought transformation not only in the area of housing, but also in the areas of youth and economic development.

## Youth

Relying on the BEAT process, the Ensley Forum organized the Ensley

Youth Council, a community-wide leadership council for high school youth. The Ensley Youth Council helps youth develop leadership and community problem-solving skills. It helps young people to see themselves as effective decision makers and change agents in their own lives and communities.

Youth Council members identify their own priorities, set their own agenda, and run their own meetings. They help design and participate in a year-long leadership training program, which teaches leadership, advocacy, organizing, and community problem-solving skills. Through the training, young people identify their own gifts, work collectively to take on projects successfully, learn skills related to cooperative power sharing, and work through personal issues which can derail young people—issues such as class, gender, race, self-esteem, and internalized oppression.

Youth Council members have undertaken several community improvement projects, such as helping build one of the BEAT houses and collecting Christmas toys for community children. Other activities have included visits to historically black colleges in Atlanta and Montgomery.

BEAT/Ensley Forum's Youth Committee is comprised of youth, youth agencies, parents, school teachers and administrators, and community and church leaders. The Youth Committee organizes a number of efforts designed to strengthen the academic and social achievement of community youth. Three churches provide tutoring for children of all ages. As a result, children have shown measurable improvements in their school performance. Volunteer tutors include high school and college youth, as well as persons from across racial, class and geographic lines throughout the Birmingham area.

A partnership with a suburban church provides college scholarships for Ensley youth. The scholarship program includes financial assistance which covers all of a students' individual needs, as well as mentoring and personal support. In return students are required to give back to their own community in the form of volunteer service.

A summer camp sponsored by the committee offers forty children, ages six to fourteen, a safe, challenging environment for six weeks during the summer. The camp offers a celebration of African American culture, role models for African American youth, leadership experience for high school youth who work as assistants, art and recreational activities, and exposure to social change efforts in the community. An annual parent-youth conference brings together parents and youth with many community organizations to address issues of common concern: jobs, drugs, leadership, and personal development.

## Economic Development

The Ensley Forum is working to make the Ensley economy more sustainable and more responsive to community direction. For the community this means jobs that can support a family, significant community ownership and control of the economic base, environmental integrity, and reinvestment of the community's wealth within the community. Our economic development strategy includes the following strategies.

• **Commercial Revitalization:** Ensley has suffered private and public disinvestment. Many of the commercial businesses that closed their doors did not leave Ensley because of declining profits or even because of crime. They left because aging owners lacked heirs who could continue the business; when the owner retired, the business closed. A top priority of Ensley residents is to revitalize the historic Ensley business district, emphasizing development of community- and minority-owned businesses. We are working to develop a one-stop social service center in our commercial district. We have located a youth jazz school in the commercial district, and have assisted in the creation of several resident-owned businesses. Increasing local ownership is the linchpin of our economic development strategy. We have acquired property in the downtown Ensley area and, when possible, we plan to make the property available to local owners. The city has committed to making major street improvements which will make the area safer and more inviting.

• **Industrial Redevelopment:** An abandoned industrial site represents a major economic and environmental justice concern for the Ensley community. We are working with the city to ensure that the community will have a voice in redevelopment plans for the abandoned industrial site.

• **Access to Birmingham-area Employment Opportunities:** We work with area corporations to make jobs available to Ensley residents, especially youth and young adults.

# 7

# Conclusion: What We've Done

A charge to keep, I have. A God to glorify.
A never dying soul to save and fit it for the sky
To serve this present age. My calling to fulfill.
And, may It all of my powers engage to do my Master's will.

REWEAVING the torn fabric of the former Sandy Bottom community — rent by the brokenness, distrust, neglect, hopelessness, and despair — has been a very challenging, yet gratifying experience. It has expanded my understanding of what it means to have faith and strengthened my commitment as a pastor to a ministry that is rooted in justice, compassion, and hope.

Carving out a relevant, inclusive, and community-directed ministry which produces tangible and intangible results is tough work — very tough! This type of ministry requires an incredible degree of faith, determination, and personal commitment. It cannot be done if leaders and participants are not willing to trust the abilities, gifts, and leadership of others, both inside and outside the local church and neighborhood.

Everyone, regardless of race, ethnic origin, or social and economic status, has something special and useful to bring to the table of ideas and opportunity. Creating opportunities for each person to contribute to the meaningful working relationship between individuals and organizations is the essence of community-directed ministry.

I have worked with many pastors and neighborhoods engaged in the reweaving process. Initially, there is always a great deal of excitement and hope among the leaders and participants, but as challenging issues emerge—issues ranging from personality conflicts to frustrating lack of rapid, tangible results— many become disillusioned and quit. However, thanks be to God, several church and neighborhood leaders have not given up the fight! Positive change will occur in these communities, just as it has in Sandy Vista!

That is what faith and church are all about. They are about persevering and defying the odds. They are about transformation and resurrection, not only in the lives of individuals but in entire communities as well. That is why it is important for churches to make rebuilding community a priority once again. Destructive social, economic, and political forces have all but ripped apart the very fabric of our communities, shattering the hopes and dreams of our neighbors. These forces leave in their wake dysfunctional families, children at risk, economic despair, and a growing sense of hopelessness that things will never change.

For too long, the church has been in a rather reactive mode, mourning the state of our neighborhoods but, in many cases, depending exclusively on government and other agencies and institutions to "fix the problems." There is a very important role that these entities can and should play. But any strategy that does not directly engage the active participation of people from within the needy neighborhoods cannot lead to the human development or social and economic transformation that is sorely needed in our troubled communities. Ultimately, the neighborhood must be in charge of the process. For that to happen, someone must take the lead in gathering the community and organizing its members to trust each other and work together. The local congregation can and should do this. It is what we are called by the gospel to do.

The problems facing our neighborhoods are complex and require a major infusion of human and monetary resources to improve physical and economic conditions. However, I have learned through the BEAT experi-

Ten years ago, many could not envision Avenue "D" in Ensley pictured as it is today.

ence that it is not enough for the church to build new houses or community centers, or develop new businesses and other tangible signs of progress, if there is not a deliberate and concentrated focus on building community. The church must promote creation of a process that enables others to respect, cherish, and value our interdependency and shared vision, hopes, dreams and values. In the final analysis, this is what the BEAT process is about — reweaving the fabric of our shared humanity into a viable community where all can live in dignity and in hope.

Achieving this goal is never solely about developing a product, a house, or a program; nor is it about making a political statement. It is not about building the reputation or ego of the leaders. Rather, it is about people talking, planning and caring about one another again. It is about neighbors being neighbors, house by house, block by block, church by church, community by community.

# 8

# Making It Happen Step by Step

THIS chapter provides a step-by-step review of the community-based neighborhood development process discussed earlier in the BEAT story. We hope what you learn will help your group devise its own process. Remember that this an ongoing process—one that never stops. It includes engaging the community to generate trust and input, convening community meetings to clarify options and decide on priorities, building partnerships with people outside the neighborhood to support the efforts, and then involving the community in every step of planning and implementation. It culminates in celebrating of results; then the cycle is repeated for the next phase of the overall plan.

First, this review outlines the individual steps taken in each of two major phases of the process undertaken by BEAT. The steps are presented in the form of guidelines for those who wish to implement a similar process. Next, the housing development process in Sandy Bottom is used to illustrate how the steps are applied to a specific task.

## The BEAT Process

### Phase One: Community Building within the Neighborhood and Church

- Form a core group of five to ten people, from both the church and the neighborhood, who are committed to building new relationships within the community through regular and sustained cooperation.
- Begin walking the streets and meeting the people neighborhood. Listen to their stories and what they know about their community.
- Develop a survey and administer it door to door to community residents to deepen the conversation.
- Plan a community meeting about survey results.
- Go door to door, and tell each person when the first community meeting will be held.
- Begin announcements that a series of community meetings will be held on a regular basis (once a week or every two weeks) to create a vision for the neighborhood.
- Invite as many of the people in the neighborhood as possible. Do so repeatedly. Walk the streets again to invite people before the first meeting.
- Convene the community meetings to report survey results and promote community discussion about how to interpret the findings.
- Have a sign-in sheet at every meeting with spaces for names, addresses and phone numbers.
- Use the first meeting as an occasion for people to introduce themselves and to relate their history in the community. Ask them to describe their hopes and fears. Ask for help in completing the community survey and in formulating a mailing list and telephone network. Volunteers may be few at first, but do not become discouraged.
- Keep everyone talking at the first meeting. The pattern that is established here is very important. Make sure everyone gets a chance to talk. Do not let a few people dominate. If needed, pro-

pose a system in which each person gets a turn before another person speaks a second time. Establish as a ground rule that everyone's input is needed.

- Encourage the group to begin and end with prayer and to pray when they hit hard spots in the conversation.
- Continue community meetings to identify priorities and action steps.
- Assess the needs.
- Identify available and needed resources.
- Develop a mission statement.
- Identify members for the board of directors.
- Form a nonprofit corporation.
- Identify an attorney, and develop bylaws and articles of incorporation.
- Apply for 501(c)(3) IRS status to secure tax-exemption.
- Hold board development seminars.
- Engage in strategic planning.
- Use regular community meetings to examine the strengths, weaknesses, opportunities, and threats to the neighborhood. This task may require several meetings.
- Look for skills that each participant brings. Begin to suggest ways for them to be involved. Be direct and ask individuals to handle specific needs.
- Identify three to five top priorities to address. Take a meeting to discuss each one.
- Identify short-term and long-term action steps on each priority.
- Develop an action plan. [See Appendix C for BEAT's action plan.]
- Take action on the short-term goals while the vision clarification process is still going on.
- Form a work group to address each priority, and identify a leader for the group.
- Work groups/committees should include but not be limited to the following:

  *1. Community Organizing:* Tasks include organizing community residents and outreach, including, marketing, publicity, and producing a monthly newsletter.

*2. Housing:* Tasks include construction, land acquisition, security, maintenance, family section, mortgages, property management, and site preparation.

*3. Finance:* Tasks include fund raising, grant preparation, budgeting, accounting, and operations

*4. Education:* Tasks focus on enhancing the community's capacity to direct its own future and include designing retreats, workshops, and leadership development and capacity-building sessions.

*5. Personnel:* Tasks include identifying and selecting needed volunteer and paid staff.

*6. Strategic Planning and Board Development:* Tasks include oversight of the strategic planning process and identifying and liaising with board members.

## Phase Two: Share the Vision and Enlist the Community.

•     Contact neighborhood leaders, city council members, and the heads of city or county government departments (e.g., economic development, housing, education, planning, law enforcement, human services, and industrial recruitment). Ask for representatives to participate in your core group meetings and the community meetings you plan.

•     Set up meetings with the directors of any religious and social service agencies, as well as other denominational leaders in the area, and ask for representation in your core group.

•     Contact media representatives in your area.

•     Establish contact with the managers of banks in the neighborhood.

•     Meet business leaders in the area.

•     Become acquainted with area school principals.

•     Propose a working partnership with government, business, social service, education, and religious groups you encounter. Ask for a representative to participate.

•     Publish a very small and informal newsletter, which updates readers on plans and progress, about one-third of the way through the community meetings series. Schedule a second issue about two-thirds of the way. Disseminate the newsletter to as many people as possible.

• Assist work group leaders in locating the governmental, professional or financial resource people needed to assist the group in their work.

• Report back to the community and to social service, governmental, financial and religious groups that you have met. Be open and realistic about the community's plans and needs.

• Ask religious groups in particular to help support the process with working funds and some staff support for mailings, and the like. Funds for operational expenses are the most difficult to locate, and donated resources can help cover shortfalls.

• Encourage committee leaders to keep the work groups meeting.

• Report work groups' progress and needs to a full neighborhood meeting at least once a month.

• Make sure short-term actions are taken. Report both actions and accomplishments, no matter how small, to the community.

• Publish priorities and short- and long-term goals, along with other results of the community survey and neighborhood meetings, in a special edition of the newsletter.

• Celebrate the priorities, and hold a worship service to ask for God's blessings on them. Invite the entire community and representatives from government, schools, businesses, churches, and social service agencies.

• Take priorities to the governmental leaders of the area, and ask for direct help in carrying out the community's plans. Be open and flexible about ways to help achieve the goals, but insist on the community's priorities and involvement at every stage.

• Share community priorities with to the managers of the branch bank and other major businesses in the area. Be optimistic about their÷ involvement, but expect it to take time. Ask for specific, feasible, short-term, direct help.

• Ask for support from both the news and marketing departments of local media .

• Look for contacts with people who have a historical connection with the neighborhood (*e.g.,* folks who may have grown up there).

•      Keep the work groups for each priority task meeting regularly and making plans for action.

•      Announce the first major strategy to tackle one of the biggest priorities. Make sure the strategy has manageable, short-term action steps that lead to bigger actions within six months to two years.

•      Keep the conversation going with all of the partner groups.

•      Continue newsletter and informational mailings.

•      Have confidence that change will occur and progress will be made even though you may experience frustration at times if significant movement on major priorities does not occur rapidly. Government leaders and church groups will probably be the first to provide major support for proposed actions, but continue to communicate to others (e.g., banks, businesses) that you expect their participation.

•      Continue to plan and carry out short-term actions steps.

•      Be ready to approach banks and businesses as soon as the first contributions and support commitments come in. Businesses rarely want to be the first to commit, but they are often responsive to tangible evidence of emerging credible partnerships.

•      Don't give up when your faith and the community's faith are inevitably tested. There will be times when you will feel that nothing is going to happen. BEAT's experience suggests that this is a sign that you have engaged forces or encountered barriers that keep the neighborhood down.

•      Plan worship services and community gatherings. Bring people together as much as possible. Don't be surprised if some people drop out because things are not moving fast enough for them.

•      Plan some musical gatherings and events for youth and the elderly. Minister to the community, and keep their hope alive.

•      See what God will do.

•      As support begins to come in, make sure the community is present for all meetings.

•      Celebrate the small things, and keep telling the community's stories and highlighting priorities.

•      Get ready for things to move faster than you can handle.

- Anticipate increased need for staff to keep things organized.
- Focus on keeping the community organized and informed as the first priority in the midst of other increasing demands.
- Connect supporters and contributors from outside of the neighborhood to everyone in your work groups and not just to one or two leaders in the core group.
- Keep meeting, planning, and acting.
- As a leader, never go anywhere on organization business by yourself.
- Remember that the first key steps are likely to be taken by the people in the neighborhood rather than by outside helpers.

## Applying the BEAT Process to Housing Development

BEAT has come to believe that housing is an essential component to community revitalization. We recognize, however, that every neighborhood will set its own priorities, and we believe the BEAT process will allow any neighborhood to do so. Since housing development played such a major role in our case, it provides a good illustration of how the BEAT planning and implementation process can be applied to specific needs. The guidelines presented below reflect the sequence of events in BEAT's housing initiative.

## Financing and Preparation Phase

- Identify development team: church members, residents, architects, planners, engineers, city officials, contractors.
- Determine scope of project area.
- Define all costs.
- Identify property owners.
- Get appraisals on all property.
- Have city officials declare targeted area an urban renewal district.
- Obtain from neighborhood residents and partners (e.g., government, denominations, businesses, individuals) financing to acquire properties.

• Contact local neighborhood-based housing groups in your area, or elsewhere, to learn about the home ownership financing options for low-income families and individuals.

• Meet with local banking officers to discuss options for financing low-interest mortgage loans or mortgage loans secured by a nonprofit group.

• Arrange engineering studies on properties.

• Determine if there is a need rezoning, site preparation, infrastructure improvement, and soil testing.

• Determine design standards. [See Appendix for BEAT design standards.]

• Determine construction time line. [See Appendix G for Construction Critical Path Chart .]

• Determine cost of the houses that prospective owners can afford.

• Determine the "who and how" of the actual construction work.

• Identify contractor and subcontractors.

• Identify project coordinator(s). The person or persons filling this position will provide oversight and act as the organization's representative during construction. He or she will be responsible for ensuring that the work is being done properly and on time. The project coordinator must work closely with the contractor or construction manager, communicating with that person regularly and visiting the construction site frequently to track the rate of work, delivery and installation of building materials, and the inspection process.

• Identify volunteer coordinator(s). The person or persons filling this position will serve as the primary contact for all volunteer labor. He or she will recruit and coordinate volunteer construction labor, making sure that the required number of volunteers with the necessary skills, are ready and available when needed by the contractor. The volunteer coordinator must determine the best match between volunteers and the various construction tasks and work closely with the contractor to keep labor available on schedule.

• Identify a security coordinator and staff. The organization needs to identify persons who are willing to provide round-the-clock site security for the duration of construction.

- Develop a mortgage application [See Appendix F.]
- Identify mortgage holders (e.g., banks, churches, financial institutions).
- Identify potential home buyers and renters.
- Form a residents association for all current and prospective residents.
- Develop community covenants among the residents. [See Appendix H.]
- Obtain completed applications and fee for credit check from housing applicants.
- Determine if families qualify for permanent financing. BEAT submitted its applications to Neighborhood Services, Inc. (NSI), a local housing agency that provides technical assistance to other housing groups and processes credit information for BEAT. NSI counsels the family and determines whether family pre-qualifies for permanent financing.
- Assist families with financing difficulties to clear up obstacles to qualifying. Local banks can also review applications and determine if families qualify for permanent financing.
- Require qualified families to attend a series of home buyer workshops organized by local banks.
- Submit application to a lending institution.

Once the family qualifies for a BEAT-arranged mortgage, the family is accepted into the BEAT home-buying program. The family is required to:

- Attend BEAT board meetings.
- Attend Sandy Vista Residents Association meetings.
- Attend home buyer workshops.
- Participate in neighborhood programs and activities.
- Attend BEAT orientation sessions
- Provide "sweat equity" in the construction of their new home

## Construction Phase

- BEAT identifies financial sponsor(s) (e.g., church, city government, corporation) to supply construction costs and volunteer labor.

- BEAT identifies lot in the designated redevelopment area.
- BEAT pairs the family with a volunteer architect.
- Family meets with architect to provide input about the design of each new home and review design standards and community covenants.
- Complete housing design.
- Submit plans to city agencies for permits.
- Organize a ground breaking ceremony, and invite the home buyer's family, sponsoring group, BEAT members, and local residents.
- Ensure that the volunteer coordinator meets or consults regularly with the agencies or groups offering assistance.
- Develop in consultation with the construction coordinator, a volunteer work schedule that outlines the nature of the work, how long it will take to complete a particular phase, how many volunteers will be needed, and what the voluntary group need to bring to the work site.
- Coordinate the meal schedule and who will provide food.
- Begin construction.
- Keep all volunteers busy for the duration of the project.
- If there is a volunteer group& working under the supervision of a contractor, make sure that group is organized in teams, each with its own team captain. Team captains must meet regularly with the volunteer coordinator and contractor.
- Make sure that the necessary housing inspections are scheduled and carried out in a timely manner.
- Submit all documents required for closing to relevant local lending institutions.
- Schedule with the new homeowner, BEAT, and the lender an appointment for closing.
- Housing blessing ceremony.
- Family moves into new home.

## Home Purchase Closing

Typical closing scenario for a new house in Sandy Vista—1,100 to 1,300 square feet, three to four bedrooms, one-and-a half baths
- Purchase price $42,500

- Cash required at closing $1,500
- The buyer executes the first mortgage loan for $34,000 on a $42,500 house. The first mortgage is generally a thirty year mortgage financed at the current interest rate.
- The buyer executes a second mortgage loan for $8,500. The second mortgage is generally held by BEAT or the city of Birmingham. The city of Birmingham second mortgage program has a fixed mortgage rate of three percent interest for fifteen years.
- The buyer is responsible for prepaid items such as two months' hazard or homeowner's insurance premiums, fifteen days' interest, recording fees, mortgage fees, and state taxes, all of which must be paid at closing.
- The seller, BEAT, pays the remaining prepaid items not assigned to the buyer, such as survey and appraisal fees.
- Monthly mortgage notes, including taxes and insurance, on all BEAT houses do not exceed $350.

# Appendices

THIS SECTION consists of various documents and worksheets that can be used as models by a group seeking to replicate the BEAT success in their own community.

# APPENDIX A:

# NEIGHBORHOOD ASSESSMENT

*As noted earlier, the BEAT team used surveys both to gather information and to increase the awareness and feeling of participation of community residents, so that they would have a sense of ownership of the neighborhood redevelopment process. Following are some examples of the forms we used.*

# Resident Survey

*Before beginning this survey, we drew up an introduction to the survey which explained to the survey-takers why the survey was being done and how it should be administered.*

## Purpose:

The main purpose of the survey is to obtain information about certain consumer/shopping habits and to ascertain the needs in the community for consumer goods and services that might be incorporated into an economic development initiative for the community.

Further, the survey is intended to provide important demographic, socio-economic, and housing information; as well as some insight into the residents' perceptions of the neighborhood and the BEAT affordable housing initiative.

## Administration of the survey:

The survey, consisting of 20 to 30 separate questions, will be administered by volunteers from the community. It will be done by door-to-door interview, with approximately 20 minutes fro each household interview.

The answers to each question will be recorded on a standard answer sheet by each interviewer. There will be one answer sheet for each household interview. The answers will be tabulated, then analyzed by computer. The arrangements for this analysis have not been made as yet.

Except as noted below, all questions will be constructed in a way that will make the recording of answers simple and straightforward.

The survey will be administered and the data kept in such a way so as to insure anonymity of the respondents. No names or addresses will be involved.

## General Categories of the Survey Questions:

1. Family Profile:

This will involve a series of 8 to 10 questions that will reveal demographic and socio-economic information for each household. Specific questions will deal with: the number of people in the household, the age distribution of children, presence of extended family (grandparents, grandchildren, other relatives), single-headed household vs. dual-headed household, the number of wage earners in the household, the household income, and related general household information.

2. Housing Profile:

This series of 4 to 6 questions will reveal certain basic information about the housing unit occupied by each household. Questions will deal with: owner vs. renter, the total number of rooms in the unit, the number of bedrooms and bathrooms, the household's monthly payment for rent or mortgage and utilities, and other pertinent housing-related information.

3. Profile of shopping habits and needs:

This will involve 6 to 8 questions related to current shopping habits and perceived and actual needs of the household for goods and services that are not provided in the community. The questions will deal with: the extent to which the household shops in downtown Ensley at present and the array of goods and services obtained in the community, what would be necessary in order for the household to do more shopping in the community, and the array of goods and services that should be provided in the community.

This portion of the survey will also address issues related to the need for day care services, and other as yet undefined services as well.

4. Attitudes and perceptions about the neighborhood:

This last portion of the survey will involve 4 simple questions that will reveal certain household attitudes about the neighborhood. Respondents will be asked to list 3 things that they like about the neighborhood and 3 things that they dislike. These will be the only 2 questions that will involve specific written answers on the survey answer sheet.

The respondents will also be asked about the extent to which they think the BEAT project will benefit the community and themselves personally.

*The survey instrument was as follows:*

## Part A: Family Profile

1. How many people live permanently in your residence?
        ( ) one
        ( ) two
        ( ) three
        ( ) four
        ( ) five
        ( ) six
        ( ) seven
        ( ) eight
        ( ) more than eight

2. How many separate households live in your residence?

  ( ) one

  ( ) two

  ( ) three

  ( ) more than three

3. How many children under the age of 18 live in your residence?

  ( ) none

  ( ) one

  ( ) two

  ( ) three

  ( ) four

  ( ) five

  ( ) six

  ( ) more than six

4. How many children in the residence are currently in elementary or secondary school?

  ( ) none

  ( ) one

  ( ) two

  ( ) three

  ( ) four

  ( ) five

  ( ) six

  ( ) more than six

5. Is there an extended family in your residence?

  ( ) no

  ( ) yes, grandparent or grandparents

  ( ) yes, grandchildren

  ( ) yes, other relatives

6. How many full or part-time wage earners presently live in your residence?

  ( ) one

  ( ) two

  ( ) three

  ( ) four

( ) more than four

7. What is the total yearly income of the primary or principal wage earner in the principal household?

    ( ) less than $7,500/year
    ( ) $7,500 to 10,000/year
    ( ) $10,000 to 12,500/year
    ( ) $12,500 to 15,000/year
    ( ) $15,000 to 17,500/year
    ( ) $17,500 to 20,000/year
    ( ) $20,000 to 25,000/year
    ( ) $25,000 to 30,000/year
    ( ) over $30,000/year

8. What is the total yearly income of all wage earners that live in your residence?

    ( ) less than $7,500/year
    ( ) $7,500 to 10,000/year
    ( ) $10,000 to 12,500/year
    ( ) $12,500 to 15,000/year
    ( ) $15,000 to 17,500/year
    ( ) $17,500 to 20,000/year
    ( ) $20,000 to 25,000/year
    ( ) $25,000 to 30,000/year
    ( ) over $30,000/year

## Part B: Housing Profile

1. Do you own or rent your residence?

    ( ) own
    ( ) rent

2. How many rooms are in your residence (excluding kitchen and bathrooms)?

    ( ) one
    ( ) two
    ( ) three
    ( ) four

( ) five

( ) six

( ) more than six

3. How many bedrooms does your residence have?

( ) one

( ) two

( ) three

( ) four

( ) five

( ) more than five

4. How many bathrooms does your residence have?

( ) one

( ) two

( ) three

( ) more than three

5. What is the monthly payment for rent or mortgage for your residence?

( ) less than $100/month

( ) $100 to 150/month

( ) $150 to 200/month

( ) $200 to 250/month

( ) $250 to 300/month

( ) $300 to 350/month

( ) $350 to 400/month

( ) $400 to 450/month

( ) $450 to 500/month

( ) more than $500/month

6. What is your average monthly cost for all utilities

( ) none (included in rent)

( ) less than $100/month

( ) $100 to 125/month

( ) $125 to 150/month

( ) $150 to 150/month

( ) $150 to 175/month

( ) $175 to 200/month

( ) more than $200/month

## Part C. Shopping Habits and Needs

1. Do you or members of your family shop in downtown Ensley?

      ( ) never

      ( ) 1 or 2 times a month

      ( ) 1 time per week

      ( ) more than 1 time per week

2. Which goods and services do your normally obtain in downtown Ensley?

      ( ) groceries

      ( ) convenience goods

      ( ) cleaners

      ( ) drug store

      ( ) shoes

      ( ) shoe repair

      ( ) gas/auto products

      ( ) auto repair

      ( ) clothes

      ( ) clothing repair

      ( ) fast food

      ( ) furniture

      ( ) other repairs

      ( ) other goods/services (please list)

3. Which goods and services would you likely obtain in downtown Ensley if they were available?

      ( ) groceries

      ( ) convenience goods

      ( ) cleaners

      ( ) drug store

      ( ) shoes

      ( ) shoe repair

      ( ) gas/auto products

      ( ) auto repair

      ( ) clothes

      ( ) clothing repair

( ) fast food

( ) furniture

( ) other repairs

( ) other goods/services (please list)

4. Do you think that downtown Ensley is a safe place to shop and spend time during the day?

( ) yes

( ) no

5. Would you shop more frequently in downtown Ensley if a greater variety of shops and merchants were in the area?

( ) yes, important

( ) yes

( ) no

6. Would you shop more frequently in downtown Ensley if the area looked better, and was cleaner and neater in appearance?

( ) yes, important

( ) yes

( ) no

7. Would you shop more frequently in downtown Ensley if you thought it were a safer place?

( ) yes, important

( ) yes

( ) no

8. Do you presently use day care services?

( ) no

( ) yes, 1/2 day

( ) yes, full day

( ) yes, extended day

9. Would you be likely to use day care services if such services were available in the SandyVista neighborhood?

( ) no

( ) yes, 1/2 day

( ) yes, full day
( ) yes, extended day

## Part D.  Neighborhood Attitudes and Perceptions

1. List three things that you especially like about your neighborhood.

_____

_____

_____

2. List three things that you especially dislike about your neighborhood.

_____

_____

_____

3. How safe do you feel in your neighborhood?
    ( ) always safe
    ( ) generally safe, but occasionally unsafe
    ( ) occasionally safe, but often unsafe
    ( ) generally unsafe
    ( ) very unsafe and fearful
4. How enthusiastic are you about the BEAT housing initiative?
    ( ) very
    ( ) somewhat
    ( ) don't care
5. Do you think the BEAT housing initiative will benefit the neighborhood?

( ) yes, greatly

( ) yes, somewhat

( ) no

6. Do you think the BEAT housing initiative will benefit you personally, or your family?

( ) yes, greatly

( ) yes somewhat

( ) no

7. Would you be interested in obtaining a new or renovated house through the BEAT program?

( ) yes

( ) no

*In February 1993, we used the following survey form to find out how people were feeling about the changes in the neighborhood:*

# Sandy Vista Community Survey

1. If you lived in the "Sandybottom" community before BEAT started its work in 1990, on a scale of "1" thru "10" how would you have rated the community then?

1   2   3   4   5   6   7   8   9   10

*Please explain.

2. On a scale of "1" thru "10" how do you feel about the neighborhood now?

1  2  3  4  5  6  7  8  9  10

*Please explain.

3.  If you lived here at the time BEAT started re-developing this community, did you really expect the neighborhood would be improved?
__ Yes
__ No
__ Unsure
*Comments _____

4.  What would you consider to be major problem areas in this community, right now?  Please rank according to importance.
   "1" very important     "2" important
__Drug Abuse
__Unemployment
__Lack of Community Recreation
__Safety
__Alcohol Abuse
__Lack of Educational Programs
__Pharmacy
__Others: _____

5.  If a new business was started in this community, what kind of business would be most helpful to you, right now?  Please rank according to importance.
   "1" very important     "2" important
__Supermarket
__Laundromat
__Day Care Center
__Child Development Center
__Restaurant
__Clothing Store
__Convenience Store

\_\_Barber/Beauty Shop
\_\_5 and 10 Store
\_\_Others: _____

6. If a group of your neighbors and BEAT wanted to create a community owned business, would you be interested in joining them?
\_\_Yes
\_\_No

7. What kind of business would you like to be a part of if you had the opportunity?

_____

8. What kind of work-related skills do you possess?

_____

9. What do you think is the most important thing BEAT should work on next?

_____

10. Is there anything else BEAT should be thinking about?

_____

# APPENDIX B: TIME LINES AND ACTION PLANS

*With as many volunteers and residents involved, it was critical to have timelines and schedules that kept everyone involved and moving ahead. Following is a sample of one of our action plans. Note the number of different people involved in the various committees.*

B.E.A.T.'s ACTION PLAN
1991
COMMITTEE ACTIVITY

| COMMITTEE ACTIVITY | COORDINATORS | |
|---|---|---|
| 1. **DEDICATION PROGRAM** <br> Bethel A.M.E. Church <br> 3:00 p.m., 3/24/91 <br><br> Target Date:  2/28/91 | 1. Program Chairperson <br> 2. Publicity Chairperson <br> 3. Speakers <br> 4. Gov't Reps <br> 5. Ground Breaking Activity <br> 6. Invitation Committee | Treva Rice <br> Ronald Nored <br> C. Brown <br> C. Brown <br> Ray Harris <br> Treva Rice |
| 2. **PUBLICITY** (News Media, etc.) | 1. Contact Person | Ronald Nored |
| 3. **RESUBDIVISION OF LOTS** <br> (Identify Engineering Survey Company) <br> a. City of Birmingham – Victor Blackledge <br> b. Miller, Triplett & Miller – Joe Miller, (Per Al Rosen) <br> c.  CB, Inc. – Dara Thornton, (Per Dick Pigford) <br> d.  Shoal Engineering | 1. Coordinators | Ronald Nored <br> C. Brown <br> Ray Harris <br> Al Rosen |
| 4. **DEFINE HOUSING DESIGN** <br> (Tuesday Group will begin to design houses for: <br> a. Total Avenue D Block <br> b.  Promotion presentation for the Dedication Ceremony) <br> Need Pictures, etc.  The following generic design is recommended: <br> 1000 sq. ft.; 2 to 3 bedrooms; 1 or 2 full baths; living room; <br> kitchen with family room combination; dining room; porch; driveway; <br> carport, if possible; small storage and wash room. | 1. Contact Persons <br> 2. Target Dates <br>   3/24/91 – Drawings <br>     Completed <br>   4/1/91 – Meet with Family <br>   5/1/91 – Building Start  James Scott | Ray Harris <br> C. Brown <br> Ronald Nored <br><br> Frank Setzer <br> * <br> Dick Pigford <br> Al Rosen |
| 5. **CHECK ON EXISTING SANITARY SEWAGE** <br> (for intial building site (legal description may be needed) | | Al Rosen <br> Ronald Nored <br> C. Brown |
| 6. **CHECK GRADING REQUIREMENTS** <br>    Victor Blackledge or Engineering Dept, City of Birmingham | | C. Brown |
| 7. **TARGET FIRST FAMILY FOR FIRST HOUSE** | | Ray Patterson <br> Ronald Nored <br> Treva Rice <br> Betty Benion |
| 8. **SECURE DEMOLITION COMPANY** <br> Secure Needed Permits; Water Works, Sewage, Gas, Electricity, etc. | | C. Brown <br> Ronald Nored <br> Al Rosen |
| 9. **IDENTIFY LIST OF MATERIALS NEEDED TO BUILD 1000 Sq. Ft. HOUSE** (Check Alto Tarver of NSI) | | C. Brown <br> C. Brown <br> Ronald Nored <br> Al Rosen |

# Appendix C: Sample Grant Application

*As BEAT began to develop its mission and move into the early stages of redevelopment, the need for funding was critical. By carefully describing who we were, what we were trying to accomplish, and how we were going about it, we succeeded in obtaining several substantial grants from foundations, government agencies, religious organizations, and corporations. Following is a typical grant application.*

BEAT
1524 Avenue D Ensley
Birmingham, Alabama 35218
(205) 780-4352

## A. ORGANIZATION DESCRIPTION:

BEAT is a community transformation effort which organizes low income residents to restore the Sandy Bottom neighborhood, one of the so-called "dying neighborhoods" in the inner-city, into a healthy and growing community. Since 1990, BEAT has constructed 30 low-cost homes for ownership and rental use. The goal is to redevelop a six-block area with 64 new affordable homes. A wide array of organizations have joined in the effort, including churches which provide labor, funds and technical assistance; businesses which donate materials, equipment and technical resources; and the City of Birmingham which has provided technical assistance and almost $2 million in infrastructure and financing through housing bond funds. A Board of Directors predominated by low-income African-American residents has given leadership to the entire effort. BEAT has also organized a residents' association which works to sustain and uplift the neighborhood.

## B. PROJECT DESCRIPTION:

In the process of redeveloping the Sandy Bottom neighborhood, now renamed Sandy Vista, residents gained confidence in their capacity to reclaim their community. They began to look at some of the more systemic problems facing them.

Out of this process was born the Ensley Community Issues Forum. A project of BEAT, the Ensley Forum organizes low income residents to work on economic development and youth issues. Churches, neighborhood associations, social service agencies, businesses, schools and residents have been convened by Ensley Forum to do the work of community transformation. Short-term goals include organizing the community to develop a One-Stop Service Center as a linchpin for commercial revitalization, expand our job bank and job training programs, and organize and empower youth through Ensley Youth Council.

## A1. ORGANIZATION HISTORY AND MISSION

BEAT/Ensley Forum is a community organizing and development effort in Ensley, a low income neighborhood in Birmingham, Alabama. BEAT has transformed the Sandy Bottom neighborhood, one of the so-called "dying neighborhoods" in the inner-city, into a healthy and growing community. The approach has been to organize low income residents and church members to reclaim their community. Since 1990, BEAT has constructed 30 affordable homes for ownership and rental use. A residents' association works to sustain and uplift the neighborhood. A wide array of organizations participate in the effort, including churches which provide labor, funds and technical assistance; businesses which donate materials, labor, equipment and technical resources; and the City of Birmingham which has provided technical assistance and over $2 million in infrastructure, land acquisition, site preparation, construction, landscaping and financing through housing bond funds. A Board of Directors predominated by low-income African-American residents leads the entire effort.

BEAT organized the Ensley Forum to convene the community for neighborhood restoration and renewal.

## A2. PROJECT DESCRIPTION

The Ensley Forum, a project of BEAT, organizes and equips low income residents to determine the community's future. Ensley Forum works on community organizing, economic development and youth leadership development.

Low income residents, churches, neighborhood associations, social service agencies, businesses, and schools have been convened by BEAT to carry out the work of community transformation. Short-term goals include organizing the community to develop a One-Stop Service Center as a linchpin for commercial revitalization, complete construction of a multi-purpose community center, create a School-to-Work program, and organize and empower youth through an Ensley Youth Council. We continue leadership development and facilitation for low income residents who participate in BEAT/Ensley Forum, Ensley Youth Council and Sandy Vista Residents' Association.

## A4. DESCRIPTION OF THE COMMUNITY TO BE SERVED

Ensley is a low income, African-American neighborhood in Birmingham, Alabama. Until the closing of the U.S. Steel Ensley Works, Ensley was a thriving working-class, biracial community. The closing of U.S. Steel left the community marked by poverty, decay and an abandoned, contaminated industrial site. The population is 16,500 persons, 84% of whom are African-American, 16% white. The per capita income is $6,957, less than half of the metropolitan income. Eighteen percent of the households earn less than $5,000 annually. The poverty rate for African-Americans is 35%; for whites, 16%. Almost 40% of the households are headed by females. Unemployment in 1990 was 6.9% for the wider Ensley area; 21.7% for the Tuxedo neighborhood, home of Tuxedo public housing community. Twenty percent of the households have no one employed.

## B1 & 2. MEMBERSHIP and BOARD OF DIRECTORS

BEAT has a 20-member Board of Directors, a majority of whom are low income residents. The Board gives direction to the staff, guides the overall program development, and actively participates in all areas of work of BEAT and the Ensley Forum. The Ensley Forum has its own Board, comprised of 21 representatives from low income neighborhoods, churches, schools, local businesses and social service agencies. Both Boards meet monthly. Ensley Forum has two active committees: Youth and Economic Development. The committees guide the agenda. Their work is facilitated by staff members. They are comprised of board members and volunteers. Over 200 people who live and work in Ensley have participated in a series of long-range community planning meetings.

During 1997, the Ensley Forum will become a membership-based project of BEAT. It will have its own Board of Directors, elected by its membership. The Ensley Forum Board will elect its officers (President, Vice-President, Secretary, Treasurer). The President and Vice-President will serve on the BEAT Board of Directors. Under this structure, the Ensley Forum membership at any time can vote to become a separate 501(c)3 corporation.

Members include organizations which: 1) support the Ensley Forum's mission statement; 2) are located in Ensley or represent/serve Ensley residents; 3) pay annual dues; 4) participate in work of committees. Members have the right to elect the board, vote on annual policy and priority decisions, approve changes in bylaws, and participate in all Ensley Forum Board meetings, committees and organizing efforts.

Associate members include: a) individuals who support the mission; and b) organizations which support the mission but do not work or live in Ensley. Associate members can participate in all Ensley Forum actions, meetings and discussions; they have voice but no formal vote.

The Ensley Forum will have a 15-member Board. Member organizations elect 12. Two Board seats will be reserved for youth representatives. The Board may appoint 3 diversity seats (for example, if churches or low income residents or youth are not adequately represented, the Board may appoint representatives). The Board appoints technical advisors as needed. Board terms will be three years; board members can serve consecutive terms. Terms will be staggered so that no more than 1/3 of the Board will change in any given year.

Dues for member organizations are a minimum of $50 up to $500 per year. Associate members make a contribution according to their own ability to pay.

## B3. LEADERSHIP AND STAFF DEVELOPMENT

Leadership development and capacity-building happen every time low income residents prepare for a foundation site visit, a meeting with the Mayor, or a negotiating session with a land owner. We view all of the work we do with youth from tutoring to organizing a community youth council, as critical leadership development work.

BEAT/Ensley Forum are continually doing outreach to the community to identify and recruit new leaders. We train leaders through formal training and one-on- one eadership development.

BEAT/Ensley Forum will continue a series of training events on economic development, in order to equip low income residents to lead economic development efforts in Ensley. We will also make sure that other kinds of training are made available for Ensley leaders. For instance, the President of the Sandy Vista Residents Association has participated as a Fellow in the Southern Appalachian Leadership Training Program sponsored by the Highlander Center.

BEAT/Ensley Forum will hold quarterly leadership training for the middle- and high-school students who participate in the Ensley Youth Council. Ms. George Friday has worked with staff and youth to design and carry out these trainings. Additionally, local trainers will provide leadership training on conflict resolution for Youth Council members. Youth Council members will participate in leadership training through 21st Century Youth. We will continue to provide support and leadership training for the SandyVista Residents' Association.

## B4. TECHNICAL ASSISTANCE

An architectural firm and a commercial developer have been employed by the Ensley Forum to provide technical assistance and ongoing training for community residents, Board members and staff.

We have a technical advisory team of bankers, architects, attorneys, City Economic Development, Community Development and Urban Planning staff, religious leaders and community organizers. An architectural firm and a commercial developer have been employed by the Ensley Forum to provide technical assistance and ongoing training for Board and staff.

## C1. PROJECT GOALS AND EXPECTED OUTCOMES FOR GRANT YEAR

The Ensley Forum has led the community through a comprehensive long-range planning process, with the assistance of an urban planning firm employed by the City of Birmingham. The process included a series of workshops through which low income residents voiced their needs and their dreams. It has been a bottom-up, grassroots process which included hundreds of residents in the development of a new vision for Ensley. We will continually convene community residents to speak their needs, create a vision for their community, and work together to bring that vision into reality. The following goals were confirmed through the planning process:

1) Community Leadership and Organizing: to equip the community to participate effectively in decisions which affect the community.

All of our efforts are grounded in a commitment to build the community's capacity to direct its own future. For this reason our process is very inclusive. Leadership development, outreach and organizing efforts are given a great deal of energy and attention. We convene and facilitate the work of residents, merchants, church and community leaders as they seek to transform the community, particularly in the areas of housing, economic development, youth, and human services. Through our organizing, we seek to strengthen and build collaborative relationships among existing community institutions. In some cases, needed community institutions are lacking and the Ensley Forum plays the role of catalyst. For example, while commercial revitalization is a top priority of Ensley residents, there has been no merchants' association for the Ensley business district. The Ensley Forum has organized the Ensley Merchants' Association in order to support a growing sector of African- American merchants, to help them work collaboratively with long-time white merchants, and to help them become leaders in community revitalization. For the first time, thanks to the Ensley Forum process, relationships between low income residents and local merchants are cooperative. The strengthening of these relationships and the equipping of African-American business owners to participate in the revitalization process are essential for community transformation. The Ensley Forum will continue to staff the Merchants' Association as needed.

2) Economic Development: to develop a sustainable local economy with good jobs, viable businesses, and increased community ownership and control.

We seek to make the Ensley economy more sustainable and self-directed. A sustainable economy means family-supporting jobs, community ownership and control of the economic base, environmental integrity and reinvestment of the community's wealth within the community. Our economic development strategy includes:

a) Commercial Revitalization: While Ensley has suffered private and public disinvestment, that only tells part of the story. Many of the commercial businesses which closed their doors not because of declining profits or crime. Many closed because aging owners lacked any heirs; when they retired, the businesses closed.

A top priority of Ensley residents is to revitalize the 19th Street commercial district, emphasizing development of community- and minority-owned businesses. We are working to develop a one-stop social service center in our commercial district. We also hope to locate a youth jazz institute in the commercial district. This is particularly exciting because Ensley is the home of Tuxedo Junction, made famous by the jazz great Erskine Hawkins. Thus the project links economic development, youth enrichment, and uplifting our cultural heritage. There are a number of other commercial possibilities which we will pursue in the coming year.

Our strategy is to acquire property in the downtown Ensley area and, with the help of public and private contributions, make the property available to a combination of local and outside businesses. We have a strong team assembled to assist us with this task, including architects, real estate agents, lenders and developers. The City has made a commitment to partner with us throughout the process.

b) Community planning for brownfield redevelopment: An abandoned industrial site represents a major economic and environmental justice concern for the community. We have negotiated a seat at the table with USX Corporation, Metropolitan Development Board and the City of Birmingham, so that the community will have a voice in redevelopment plans for the abandoned USX industrial site. A feasibility study has already identified improvements which must be made for the property to be marketable. An environmental assessment of the site is currently being conducted. When it is completed, we will advocate for community-driven redevelopment.

c) School-to-Work: Job training and job creation are key concerns for the Ensley community. Low income residents, parents, youth and school officials will be organized to advocate with local industry to target job creation and training to Ensley residents.

3) Youth Organizing: to organize and train youth to become community leaders.

BEAT/Ensley Forum have organized the Ensley Youth Council, a community-wide leadership council for high school youth. The Ensley Youth Council organizes youth to deal collectively with problems facing them and their communities. Through the Youth Council, young people develop leadership and community problem-solving skills. They have regular leadership training programs which help them to become effective decision-makers and change agents in own lives and communities.

Youth Council members help design and participate in a year-long leadership training program. Trainings teach leadership, advocacy and organizing skills. Through the trainings, young people identify their own skills, work collectively to take on projects successfully, learn the skills of cooperative power sharing, work with personal issues which can derail young people such as class, gender, race, self-esteem, and internalized oppression.

They have identified a social change agenda for their community, including:

1) improvement of school facilities (students struggle to study and learn while wearing coats and gloves in freezing, crumbling and rat-ridden classrooms with outdated and broken equipment); 2) development of after- school opportunities, including jobs, cultural experiences and recreation (for one example, the entire western section of Birmingham has no movie theatre); and development of youth-owned businesses.

Youth Council members have undertaken several community improvement projects, such as working on one of the BEAT houses. They have made site visits at historically black colleges in Atlanta and Montgomery.

BEAT/Ensley Forum has a Youth Committee is comprised of parents, school teachers and administrators, community and church leaders, youth agencies and youth. The Youth Committee organizes a number of efforts designed to empower community youth. Three churches provide tutoring for children of all ages. A partnership with a local church provides college scholarships for Ensley youth. A summer camp offers 40 children, ages 6 to 14, cultural and leadership experiences. An annual Parent-Youth conference organizes parents and youth to address issues of common concern: jobs, drugs, leadership and personal development.

4) Human Services: to improve access to transportation, health care and other human services.

The development of the One-Stop Social Service Center is a primary effort in this area. The One-Stop will provide residents with convenient access to utility payment and counseling services, public services, and service-oriented businesses. It will serve as a linchpin in our commercial revitalization strategy.

We participate in Citizens for Transit because poor public transportation is a major obstacle for Ensley residents trying to get to work, to public services, or to shop. We also participate in Alabama Arise, a statewide coalition working to preserve the social safety net.

5) Housing & Community Development: to create affordable housing for rental and homeownership, and to develop leadership and community among residents of that housing.

BEAT will continue to construct affordable housing and a multipurpose community center in the Sandy Vista neighborhood, toward its goal of 64 units in a 6 block area.

C2. Long-range goals

Tangible goals include physical improvement of the 19th Street area; the opening of new businesses in the commercial district; establishment of

a One- Stop Social Service Center. Less tangible but equally critical outcomes include a Merchants' Association with growing membership, working in partnership with low income neighborhoods to revitalize the area;
low income Board members equipped to give leadership to a community
economic development strategy; an increased literacy among residents
about how economic change happens; a working partnership between the
Ensley Forum, the larger community, City government and the private
sector; increased staffing with economic development expertise; broad
resident participation in committees and community forums; an active
Ensley Youth Council; improved school performance for youth; enhanced
educational, leadership and economic opportunities for youth; strengthened bonds of community.

Systemic change is a goal of Ensley Forum. In a depressed community
like Ensley, one way to accomplish systemic change is to create a new
alternative that works, something that people can see and touch and experience as a better way of life. BEAT has done just that. BEAT has re-
claimed a community. Its process has changed many institutions across
the city, public and private. The tangible product — high quality affordable housing — combined with BEAT's inclusive process have led to
change among our public and private partners. For instance, BEAT has
changed the way in which the City works with neighborhood-based efforts. The City is less paternalistic and responds more constructively to
neighborhood-driven strategies. One sign of this is that the City has recognized BEAT/Ensley Forum as the primary economic and community
development vehicle in the Ensley community. BEAT has received operating funds from UDAG grants, a first for the City. Because of BEAT's
success, foundations and the City have supported other church/commu-
nity-based revitalization efforts, projects which replicate the BEAT model
and whose leaders have been mentored by BEAT. The Ensley Forum is
using the same process to address the issues of economic development and
youth. The process has already proven to create tangible positive change
and lasting relationships among diverse groups across the city. The process
has evoked lasting change in the Ensley community and among our public
and private partners throughout Birmingham. Implementation Plans

1) Community Leadership and Organizing:

Summer: Leadership development training through Board retreat for in-depth training on community revitalization. Commercial developer will provide "on- the-job" training for the Board and staff on community revitalization (see #2 below). Organize working committees to begin implementation of long-range plan (housing, services, youth, economic development). Call participants in long-range planning process to encourage their participation in working committees. Organize community forums to work with architecture firms designing improvements for Ensley business district. Work with merchants' and neighborhoods to plan activities which will mobilize the community around revitalization efforts.

Fall: Organize community-wide meeting to report on community revitalization process and encourage broad involvement. Recruit new Youth Council members at the beginning of the school year. All quarters: Ongoing outreach through schools, churches, businesses, agencies and neighborhoods to encourage broad involvement. One training/quarter on leadership and/or community economic development. Participate in neighborhood-sponsored activities. Provide facilitation for Merchants' Association, Sandy Vista Residents Association and Youth Council.

2) Economic Development:

Summer and Fall: Develop business plan for a mixed-used economic development project which likely will include a One-Stop Service Center and Youth Jazz Institute. Economic development consultants will assist Ensley Forum and Merchants' Association in preparing a detailed commercial development plan and in recruiting businesses to the commercial district. They will do "on-the job training" with the Board and staff so that we will have the capacity to continue this work. Seek technical assistance in assessing the implications of the environmental study of the USX brownfield site. Identify other possible industrial sites in the Ensley area. Initiate School-to-Work program for high school youth.

Winter: Fundraising and negotiations necessary to implement mixed-use economic development project.

All quarters: Facilitate the commercial revitalization efforts of the Ensley Merchants' Association. This will include seeking City condemnation and removal of abandoned, dilapidated buildings, working with the City to plan strategic street improvements, special events, developing programs to assist new local business owners and to seek outside investment in Ensley. Quarterly training for Board (see #1 above).

3) Youth Development:

Summer: Organize summer camp for community youth. Identify leadership development opportunities through summer camps for high school students, such as Twenty First Century Youth's summer experience. Work with Birmingham Urban League and other agencies to develop and begin to implement regular leadership development training program for Youth Council.

Fall: Assist youth council in recruiting new members, identifying and developing new leaders. Hold third Parent-Youth Conference. Organize tutoring program for the new school year. Identify new students to participate in the college scholarship program. Work with building trades association to reorganize apprenticeship program for area youth and young adults.

All quarters: Leadership training for youth. Tutoring. Continued outreach for Ensley Youth Council.

4) Human Services:

Summer and Fall: Organize Human Services Committee to assess and begin implementation of recommendations of long-range plan. Development of One-Stop Service Center (see #2 above). Ongoing participation in Citizens' for Transit and Alabama Arise.

5) Housing & Community Development:

All quarters: Organize Housing Committee to explore possibilities for assisted- and elderly housing as part of overall commercial revitalization effort. Support BEAT's efforts to construct affordable housing, toward its goal of 64 units in a 6 block area. Target our housing efforts to Village Creek residents. Explore recommendations of long-range plan related to expansion of BEAT model in other parts of Ensley.

## E. BUDGET AND FUNDRAISING

The CHD grant support has enabled BEAT to leverage substantial private and public funds. We receive funds from Protective Life Corporation to employ a Youth Organizer. We receive grant support from Mary Reynolds Babcock Foundation, Fannie Mae Foundation, Unitarian Universalist Veatch Program and Needmor Fund, as well as local foundations, corporations and individuals. Over time we expect to generate growing income from development fees of housing and economic development efforts. We receive significant private commitments for our work.

The Board approves the budget and fundraising plans, and assists with fundraising in every way that they are able.

BEAT STAFF

Rev. Ron Nored serves as BEAT's Executive Director. He is the founder of the BEAT program and the pastor of Bethel AME Church, out of which BEAT originated. He has assisted five other communities in developing community/ church-based development efforts based on the BEAT model. Rev. Nored has extensive experience in community and social justice efforts, as well as experience in radio and television news reporting.

Angie Wright serves as Program Coordinator. She has 18 years of experience in community organizing and coalition-building in the South. She was founder of Alabama Arise, a statewide citizens' lobby on poverty issues. She is a candidate for ordination in the United Church of Christ.

Lisa Williams (Youth Coordinator) is an Ensley resident and the youth director at Bethel AME. She brings together youth and adults from across Ensley to address issues facing youth in our commnity.

# Appendix D-1:

# Homeowner Application

*BEAT's goal was to make home ownership available and affordable to as many residents in the community as possible. At the same time, we had to be fiscally responsible both in how we granted access to mortgage financing and in developing standards that would protect neighborhood property values in the years to come. Following are (a) examples of the forms we used for residents to apply for housing and (b) excerpts of the deed covenants that new homeowners had to agree to uphold.*

## APPLICATION FOR HOMEOWNERSHIP

DATE OF APPLICATION _____ SIZE OF UNIT WANTED _____

AREA OF BIRMINGHAM DESIRED _____

### PERSONAL INFORMATION

APPLICANT'S FULL NAME _____

DATE OF BIRTH _____ MARITAL STATUS _____

SOCIAL SECURITY NUMBER _____

DRIVER'S LICENSE NUMBER _____ STATE _____

CO-APPLICANT'S FULL NAME _____

DATE OF BIRTH _____

SOCIAL SECURITY NUMBER _____

DRIVER'S LICENSE NUMBER _____ STATE _____

OTHER RESIDENTS                    RELATIONSHIP            AGE

_____

_____

_____

## RESIDENCE HISTORY

PRESENT ADDRESS _____

TELEPHONE NUMBERS:  HOME _____ WORK _____

LENGTH OF TIME AT PRESENT ADDRESS _____ AMOUNT OF RENT $_____

LANDLORD OR MORTGAGE HOLDER _____

REASON FOR WANTING TO MOVE _____

ADDRESSES FOR THE PREVIOUS TWO YEARS (IF AT CURRENT ADDRESS LESS THAN 2 YRS)

OWNED          RENTED          DATES: FROM   TO                        LANDLORD
_____

_____

OWNED          RENTED          DATES: FROM   TO                        LANDLORD
_____

_____

## APPLICANT'S EMPLOYMENT HISTORY

EMPLOYED FULL TIME _____ PART-TIME _____ RETIRED_____

EMPLOYED BY_____

ADDRESS _____

HOW LONG _____ TELEPHONE NUMBER _____

POSITION HELD _____ DEPARTMENT _____

SUPERVISOR _____

GROSS INCOME (JOB) $ _____ OTHER INCOME/SOURCE $_____/_____

TOTAL GROSS INCOME $ _____ WORKING HOURS _____

EMPLOYMENT FOR PREVIOUS 2 YEARS (IF AT CURRENT EMPLOYER FOR LESS THAN 2 YRS.)

NAME                              ADDRESS                    PHONE #
_____

_____

## CO-APPLICANT'S EMPLOYMENT HISTORY

EMPLOYED FULL TIME _____ PART-TIME _____ RETIRED _____

EMPLOYED BY _____

ADDRESS _____

HOW LONG _____ TELEPHONE NUMBER _____

POSITION HELD _____ DEPARTMENT _____

SUPERVISOR _____

GROSS INCOME (JOB) $ _____ OTHER INCOME/SOURCE $_____/_____

TOTAL GROSS INCOME $ _____ WORKING HOURS _____

EMPLOYMENT FOR PREVIOUS 2 YEARS (IF AT CURRENT EMPLOYER FOR LESS THAN 2 YRS.)
NAME                                      ADDRESS                          PHONE #
_____

_____

## BANKING INFORMATION
*MAY BE A CREDIT UNION*

BANK (1) _____

BRANCH ADDRESS _____

CHECKING ACCOUNT # _____ NAME(S) ON ACCOUNT _____

SAVINGS ACCOUNT # _____ NAME(S) ON ACCOUNT _____

LOAN ACCOUNT # _____ NAME(S) ON ACCOUNT _____

BANK (2) _____

BRANCH ADDRESS _____

CHECKING ACCOUNT # _____ NAME(S) ON ACCOUNT _____

SAVINGS ACCOUNT # _____ NAME(S) ON ACCOUNT _____

LOAN ACCOUNT # _____ NAME(S) ON ACCOUNT _____

## CURRENT DEBTS
*CREDIT CARDS, AUTO LOANS, INSTALLMENT PAYMENTS, CHILD SUPPORT, ALIMONY, ETC.*

CREDITOR'S NAME _____

ACCOUNT NUMBER _____

BALANCE _____

MONTHLY PAYMENT _____

CREDITOR'S NAME _____

ACCOUNT NUMBER _____

BALANCE _____

MONTHLY PAYMENT _____

CREDITOR'S NAME _____

ACCOUNT NUMBER _____

BALANCE _____

MONTHLY PAYMENT _____

CREDITOR'S NAME _____

ACCOUNT NUMBER _____

BALANCE _____

MONTHLY PAYMENT _____

CREDITOR'S NAME _____

ACCOUNT NUMBER _____

BALANCE REMAINING _____

MONTHLY PAYMENT _____

## VERIFICATION OF EMPLOYMENT

NAME AND ADDRESS OF APPLICANT:

_____

_____

_____

NAME, ADDRESS AND PHONE NUMBER OF EMPLOYER:

_____

_____

_____

_____

POSITION HELD BY APPLICANT _____

DATE OF EMPLOYMENT _____

PROBABILITY OF CONTINUED EMPLOYMENT _____

RATE OF PAY (ESTIMATE IF NOT ACTUALLY PAID ON HOURLY OR ANNUAL BASIS)

          HOURLY $ _____     ANNUALLY $ _____

ADDITIONAL COMPENSATION $ _____
(ACTUAL AMOUNTS RECEIVED IN PREVIOUS 12 MONTHS FOR OVERTIME, COMMISSION, BONUS)

• IF APPLICANT IS IN MILITARY SERVICE, GIVE INCOME ON MONTHLY
  BASIS FOR:
          BASE PAY $ _____ QUARTERS & SUBSISTENCE $ _____

          FLIGHT OR HAZARD DUTY ALLOWANCE $ _____

OTHER COMMENTS_____

_____

_____

# APPENDIX D-2:

## NEIGHBORHOOD COVENANTS

*These are excerpts of the deed covenants that new homeowners had to agree to uphold.*

**Section 4.** **Temporary Structures**. No struction of a temporary character, trailer, basement, ten or shack shall be used at any time as a residence either temporary or permanently with the exception of a sales trailer during sale of homes under constructions. No storage building of any type shall be permitted unless such building is designed as part of the main residential structure and approved by Architectural Committee. There shall be no occupancy of any Single Family Residence or Duplex until the interior, exterior and landscaping is completed and the Architectural Committee has issued the certificate provided for in Article IV, Section 4, hereof.

**Section 5.** **Lighting**. All exterior lighting of house shall be in character and keeping with the general subdivision. Yard lighting shall be such that it does not shine toward and/or disturb adjoining land owners.

**Section 6.** **Satellite Receiving Dish**. No satellite receiving dish or antenna system shall be located on any lot unless its size and location has been approved in writing by the Architectural Control Committee.

**Section 7.** **Signs**. No sign of any kind shall be displayed to the public view on any Lot except one professional sign or not more than two (2) square feet, one sign of not more than four square feet advertising the property for sale or rent, or signs used by the General Contractor to advertise during the construction and sales period. All signs shall comply with any design specifications adopted by the Architectural Committee. No signs shall be nailed to trees. This provision shall not apply to the Developer so long as it own any Lots within the Property.

**Section 8.** **HVAC Equipment**.

(a)     Outside air conditioning units may not be located in the front yard. Outside air conditioning units shall be hidden from view by shrubbery, or other foliage or fencing.

(b)     No plumbing or heating vent shall be placed on the front side of the roof. All vents protruding from roofs shall be painted the same color as the roof covering.

**Section 9.** **Storage of Boats, Trailers and Other Vehicles**. No motor homes, boats, trailer, pick-up trucks, or vans can be parked or stored in any location that can be seen from the street. No wrecked automobiles, unmaintained automobiles or vehicles other than operating automobiles or vehicles shall be stored or located on any Lot.

**Section 10.    Tenants.** It shall be the responsibility of each Owner to insure that any tenant of the any Lot or portion thereof which is owned by him receives a copy of these Protective Covenants and that every lease utilized by such Owner contain a provision therein stating that every tenancy is subject to all of the terms and provisions of this Declaration. The Owner shall remain liable for the performance and observation of all terms and condition in this Declaration and for all costs of enforcing the same.

**Section 11.    Enforcement.** If a determination is made by the Architectural Committee that any of the restrictions in this Article V are being or have been violated upon any Lot, then the Architectural Committee shall so notify the Owner in writing, specifying the violation. If within thirty (30) days from such notification, the Architectural Committee shall make a second determination that sufficient progress has not been made to remedy the violation, the Architectural Committee may itself, direct such actions to be taken as shall be necessary or appropriate to remedy such violation. The Owner shall be liable for the cost and expense of all such actions, including legal fees and the Architectural Committee may treat all such costs and expenses therefor as a charge which shall become a lien of the Architectural Committee on the affected Lot enforceable by the appropriate proceedings at law or in equity.

## ARTICLE VI

## NATURE OF PROTECTIVE COVENANTS; DEFAULTS AND REMEDIES

**Section1.    Protective Covenants Running with the Land.** The foregoing Protective Covenants shall constitute a servitude in and upon the Property and insure to the benefit of and be enforceable by the Developer, its designated successors and assigns, or by any Owner and his respective heirs, successors and assigns for a term of fifty (50) years from the date this Declaration is recorded, after which time the said Protective Covenants shall automatically be extended for successive periods of ten (10) years, unless an agreement which has been signed by Owners who own two-thrids (2/3) or more of the then exsting Lots of the Property, agreeing to terminate or modify this Declaration, has been recorded in the Probate Court of Jefferson County, Alabama.

**Section 2.    Remedies for Default.** The existence of any default hereunder by any person or entity subject to the terms, conditions, covenants and restrictions of this Declaration shall give the Developer, its successors or assigns, any Owner, and/or their respective heirs, successors and assigns, in addition to all other remedies specified herein, the right to proceed at law or in equity to complete compliance with the terms of these Protective Covenants and to prevent the violation or breach of any of them.

**Section 3.    Nature of Remedies: Waiver.** All rights, remedies and privileges granted to the Developer and the Owners, their respective heirs, successors and assigns, pursuant to the provisions of this Declaration shall be deemed to the cumulative, and the exercise of any or more of them shall not be deemed to constitute an election of remedies, nor shall it preclude the party exercising the same, or any other party, from pursuing such other and/or additional rights, remedies or privileges as may be available to such party at law or in equity. The failure at any point in time to enforce any covenant or restriction shall in no event be deemed a waiver to the right thereafter to enforce any such covenant or restriction.

**Section 4.**     **No Reverter.** No restriction or provision herein is intended to be, or shall be construed as, a condition subsequent or as creating any possibility of a reverter.

## ARTICLE VII

## FUNCTION OF ASSOCIATION

**Section 1.**     **Name.** The name of the owners organization for the Property shall be Sandy Vista Owners' Association, Inc., which shall be incorporated as a not-for-profit corporation.

**Section 2.**     **Maintenance Responsibilities.** The Association may, at any time, in the discretion of the Board, without any approval of the members being required:

(a)     Maintain, install, reinstall, construct and repair all of the improvements within the Beautification Easement Areas, to include plantings and shrubbery, and to maintain, repair and operate any other easement area shown on any Lot which is not under the control or management of public utility;

(b)     Replace injured and diseased trees or other cover to the extent that the Board deems necessary for the conservation of water and soil and for aesthetic purposes; and

(c)     Do all such other acts which the Board deems necessary to preserve and protect the Property and the beauty thereof, in accordance with the general purposes specified in this Declaration.

**Section 3.**     **Other Rights of Association.** The Board shall have the right (but shall not be obligated) to provide services, the cost of which shall be paid out to the charges provided for the Article VIII hereof, and adopt rules, regulations, procedures and policies with respect to:

(a)     garbage and trash collection and removal;

(b)     motor vehicle operation;

(c)     parking of motor vehicles on streets or roads in the Property; and

(d)     such other matter including the general welfare of the Property as a whole.

ARTICLE VIII

COVENANTS FOR MAINTENANCE CHARGES

**Section 1.      Creation of the Lien and Personal Obligation of Charges.** Each Owner by acceptance of a deed to a Lot is deemed to covenant and agree to pay to the Association: (1) annual charges, and (2) special charges as herein provided. The annual and special charges, together with interest, costs and reasonable attorney's fees, shall be a charge on the land and shall be a continuing lien upon the Lot against which each such charge is made. Each such charge, together with interest, costs and reasonable attorney's fees, shall also be the personal obligation of the person who was the Owner of such property at the time when the charge become due. The personal obligation for delinquent charges shall not pass to his successors in title.

**Section 2.      Purpose of Charges.** The charges levied by the Association shall be used exclusively for (i) discharging the responsibilities of the Association, (ii) the procuring of services for the Owners, including, but not limited to, those services specified in Article VII hereof and such other services which may be approved by Members which own two-thirds (2/3) of the Lots and (iii) capital improvements to the Beautification Easement Areas for which the Association bears maintenance responsibility.

**Section 3.      Special Charges for Capital Improvements.** In addition to the annual charges, the Association may levy, in any given year, a special charge applicable to that year only for the purpose of defraying, in whole or in part, the cost of any construction, reconstruction or replacement of improvements within area the Association has maintenance responsibility for, including fixtures and personal property related thereto, provided that any such charge shall have the assent of two-thirds (2/3) of the votes of the Members (voting in person or by proxy) at a meeting duly called for this purpose.

**Section 4.      Uniform Rate of Charges.** Both annual and special charges must be fixed at a uniform rate for all Lots and may be collected on a monthly, quarterly or annual basis. Each Lot shall bear its pro rata part of the maintenance cost and shall not be entitled to reduction because all or some of the services for which the assessment is made are not being utilized by the Owner of such Lot.

**Section 5.      Date of Commencement of Annual Charges; Due Dates.** The annual maintenance charges provided for herein shall commence as to each Lot within the Property on the first day of January of each year. As to any Lot annexed into the Project during the calendar year, the annual charge shall commence on the next following January 1$^{st}$. Written notice of the annual charge shall be sent to every Owner subject thereto. The due dates shall be established by the Board. The Association shall, upon demand, and for a reasonable charge, furnish a certificate signed by an owner of the Association setting forth whether the charges on a specified Lot have been paid.

**Section 6.      Effect of Nonpayment of Charges; Remedies of the Association.** By his acceptance of title to a Lot subject to these Protective Covenants, each Owner is and shall be deemed to covenant and agree to pay the Association the charges provided for herein, and agrees to the enforcement of the charges in the manner herein specified. In the event the Association employs and attorney or attorneys for collection of any chare, whether by suit or otherwise, or to enforce compliance with or specific performance of the terms and conditions of this Declaration, or for any other purpose in connection with the breach of this Declaration, or for any other purpose in connection with the breach of this Declaration, each Owner agrees to pay reasonable attorney's fees and costs thereby incurred in addition to any other amounts due or any other relief or remedy obtained against said Owner. In the event of a default in payment of any such charge when due, in which case the charge shall be deemed delinquent, and in addition to any other remedies herein or by law provided, the Association may enforce each such obligation in any manner provided by law or in equity, or without any limitation of the foregoing, by either or both of the following procedures:

(a)     Enforcement by Suit. The Boar may cause a suit at law to be commenced and maintained in the name of the Association against an Owner to enforce each such charge or obligation. Any judgment rendered in any such action shall include the amount of the delinquency, together with interest thereon at the maximum legal rate per annum from the date of delinquency, court costs and reasonable attorney's fees in such amount as the Court may adjudge against the delinquent Owner.

(b)     Enforcement by Lien. There is hereby created a claim of lien, with power of sale, on every Lot to secure payment to the Association of any and all charges levied against any and all Owners, together with interest thereon at the maximum legal rate which may be paid or incurred by the Association in connection therewith, including reasonable attorney's fees. At any time within ninety (90) days after the occurrence of any default in the payment of any such charge, the Association, or any authorized representative may, but shall not be required to, make a written demand for payment to the defaulting Owner, on behalf of the Association. Said demand shall state the date and amount of the delinquency. Each default shall constitute a separate basis for a demand or claim of lien or a lien, but any number of defaults may be included within a single demand or claim of lien. If such delinquency is not paid within ten (10) days after delivery of such demand, or, even without such a written demand being made, the Association may elect to file a claim of lien on behalf of the Association against the property of the defaulting Owner. Such a claim of lien shall be executed and acknowledged by any officer of the Association, and shall contain substantially the following information.

1.     The name of the delinquent Owner;

2.     The legal description and street address of the lot against which claim of lien is made;

3.     The total amount claimed to be due and owing for the amount of the delinquency, interest thereon, collection costs and reasonable attorney's fees (with any proper offset allowed);

4.      That the claim of lien is made by the Association pursuant to this
        Declaration; and

5.      That a lien is claimed against said lot in an amount equal to the amount
        stated.

Upon recordation of a duly executed original or copy of such a claim of lien, and mailing
a copy thereof to said Owner, the lien claimed therein shall immediately attach and
become effective in favor of the Association as a lien upon the property against which
such was levied. Such a lien shall have priority over all liens or claims created
subsequent to the recordation of the claim of lien thereof, except only tax liens for real
property taxes on any property, charges on any property in favor of any municipal or
other governmental assessing unit, and the lien of any first or second mortgage on the
Lot. A foreclosure by such mortgagee of its lien shall operate to discharge any amounts
unpaid by a Lot Owner to the date of foreclosure. Any such lien may be foreclosed by
appropriate action in court or in the manner provided by law for the foreclosure of a
realty mortgage or trust deed as set forth by the laws of the State of Alabama, as the same
may be changed or amended. The lien provided for herein shall be in favor of the
Association and shall be for the benefit of all other Owners. The Association shall have
the power to bid in at any foreclosure sale and to purchase, acquire, hold, lease, mortgage
and convey any property. In the event such foreclosure is by action in court, reasonable
attorney's fees, court costs, title search fees, interest and all other costs and expenses
shall be allowed to the extent permitted by law. Each Owner hereby expressly waives
any objection to the enforcement and foreclosure of this lien in this manner and also
hereby expressly waives the defense of the statute of limitations applicable to the
bringing of any suit or action thereon.

**Section 7.      Subordination of the Lien to Mortgages.** The lien for the charges
provided for herein shall be subordinate to the lien of any first mortgage. The sale or
transfer of any property shall not affect the lien charged under this Article IX. The sale
or transfer of any property pursuant to mortgage foreclosure or any proceeding in lieu
thereof, however, shall extinguish the lien of such charges as to payments which became
due prior to such sale or transfer. No sale or transfer shall relive such property from
liability for any charges thereafter becoming due or from the lien thereof.

**Section 8.**      As to those Lots improved as a Duplex, the assessment shall be double
that of the amounts of Lot improved by a Single Family Residence.

## ARTICLE IX

## AMENDMENT OF DECLARATION

**Section 1.      Amendment by Association.** An amendment may be proposed by
written instrument signed by the Owners of not less than one-fourth (1/4) of the Lots

within the Property. Such proposed amendment or amendments shall be considered at a meeting of the Owners after written or printed notice of such meeting, stating the time and place thereof, and reciting the proposed amendment or amendments in reasonable detailed form, shall be mailed to the Owners not less than ten (10) days nor more than fifty (50) days, before the date set for such meeting. If mailed, such notice shall be deemed to be properly given when deposited in the United States mail, addressed to each Owner at the street address of his Lot, the postage thereon being prepaid. Any Owner may, by written waiver of notice signed by such Owner, waive such notice, and such waiver whether before or after the holding of the meeting, shall be deemed equivatlent to the giving of such notice to such Owner. At such meeting, the amendment or amendments proposed must be approved by the affirmative vote of Owners who own not less than three-fourth (3/4) of the total Lots of the Property in order for such amendment or amendments to become effective. Thereupon, such amendment or amendments to the Declaration shall be transcribed and certified by the Association as having been duly adopted and the original or executed copy of such amendment or amendments so certified and executed with the same formalities as a deed shall be recorded in the Probate Court of Jefferson County, Alabama, within twenty (20) days from the date on which the same became effective, such amendment or amendments to specifically refer to the recording identifying the Declaration. Thereafter, a copy of said amendment or amendments, in the form in which the same were placed of record, shall be delivered to all the Owners, by mailing or delivering a copy thereof shall not be condition precedent to the effectiveness of such amendment or amendments. At any meeting held to consider such amendment or amendments, the written vote of any Owner shall be recognized if such Owner is not in attendance at such meeting or represented thereat by proxy, provided such written vote is delivered at or prior to such meeting.

**Section 2.     Expansion of the Project.** The Project is adjacent or near other real property owned by the Developer. Said parcels of land or such portions as may from time to time be owned by the Developer are hereinafter referred to as the "Annexation Property". The Developer hereby reserves unto itself the right, but not the duty, to be exercised in its sole discretion at any time within ten (10) years from the date on which this Declaration is recorded in the Office of the Judge of Probate of Jefferson County, Alabama to submit the Annexation Property, or all or any portion thereof, to the provisions of this Declaration and thereby causes the same to become part of the Declaration. The right hereby reserved unto the Developer may be exercised only upon the execution by it of an amendment to this Declaration and the filing of the same for record in the Office of the Judge of Probate of Jefferson County, Alabama. Any such amendment shall expressly submit the Annexation Property, or portions thereof, as may be specifically described in such amendment, whereupon the provisions of this Declaration as either or both may then be amended, whereupon the provisions of this Declarations shall thenceforth be understood and construed as embracing the Annexation Property then and theretofore submitted to said provisions together with all improvements constructed thereon. Nothing contained herein shall legally require the Developer to submit all or any portion of the Annexation Property to the provisions of this Declaration. No Lot Owner shall have any rights whatsoever to object to the addition of the Annexation Property, or any portion thereof, to the Project, or the failure of the Developer to submit all or any portion of the Annexation Property to the Project.

**Section 3. Scrivener's Error.** Not withstanding the foregoing amendment provisions, and scriveners's error or omission may be corrected by the filing of any amendment to this Declaration consented to be Developer and any Owners or mortgagees of record directly affected by the amendment. No other Owner is required to consent to any such samendment. If there appears to be any other omissions or errors in this Agreement, scrivener's or otherwise, and such error or omission does not materially adversely affect the rights and interest of any other party, then such error or omission may be corrected by the filing of an amendment of this Declaration executed by the Developer without the consent of any other party.

# APPENDIX E: NEIGHBORHOOD DESIGN AND DEVELOPMENT STANDARDS

*Our architects wrote a document to explain the standards that the residents and board members had adopted to control new development in the community.*

# Site and Unit Standards

NOTE: All plans are subject to the review and approval by the TUESDAY GROUP acting on behalf of the BEAT board, or other Design Review Committee established by the BEAT board.

## * SITE DEVELOPMENT STANDARDS

1. LOT SIZES:
   Standard lot      : 50'x100'
   other SFD lots    : 50'x150'
   Duplex lots (corner): 57.5'x100'

2. YARDS AND SETBACKS:
A. SFD UNITS:
   front: 25'
   side: 12' on driveway side to 40' from front property line 5' min. beyond 40' line; 5' on side opposite the driveway
   rear: 30' minimum (with specific exceptions as approved)

B. DUPLEX UNITS: (all duplexes are located on corner lots)
   Front: 20'

      common side:  5' min. beyond the 32' line

      street side: 10'

      rear (driveway location): 12' for driveway to 32' from ROW line; 5' for the remainder of the lot width

### 3. FENCES:

Fences are allowed along the rear and common property lines. Fencing cannot extend beyond a point corresponding with the rear or back of the parking pad/driveway.  Fences cannot exceed 5' in height. Chain link fencing is allowed; wood fencing is allowed, but must conform to approved design alternatives.

### 4. PARKING PADS:

All units must have a parking pad or driveway that is 9' wide and which extends 40 feet from the front property line.

### * UNIT PROGRAM STANDARDS

1. Three bedroom (SFD) units should be in the range of 1100sf, and cannot exceed 1150sf.  These units can have only one full bath, no 1/2 baths are allowed.

2. Four bedroom (SFD) units should be in the range of 1250sf and cannot exceed 1300sf.  These units must have two full baths.

3. All duplex units must be in the range of 720 to 760sf.  Each unit must have two bedrooms and one bath.

### * UNIT DESIGN STANDARDS

A.  GENERAL (for all units):

1. All structures are limited to one story in height.

2.  All units must have a front porch.  Size and configuration are variable depending on the requirements for the specific unit and the client.

3.  The front or main entrance to each unit must be from the front

porch.

4. Each unit must have a second access/exit, or back door, this should be from the kitchen and should directly access the parking pad/driveway.

5. All units must have the finished floor elevated at least 30" above finished grade. The finished floor elevation may exceed 30" depending on the particular circumstances of the site and the unit.

6. Each unit must have a secured, at–grade storage area of approximately 50sf. The storage area should be accessible from the parking pad/driveway, or located at the rear of the structure.

7. Each unit will have a security system, as per arrangements by the BEAT board.

B. PORCH (for all units):

8. Porch size and configuration are variable depending on the requirements for the specific unit and the client

9. Porch details (e.g. piers, columns, railings, construction details, et.al), can vary, but must be selected from an array of approved alternatives.

10. Special design and construction details for porches are allowed, but must be approved.

11. The crawl space under porches must be covered with latticework.

C. FOUNDATIONS (for all units):

12. Foundations must be 8"x8"x16" standard CMU on reinforced concrete footings, sized as required. Exceptions are allowed, but must be approved.

13. Exposed foundation walls must have brick veneer.

D. ROOFS (for all units):

14. All principal roofs must be gable–end. Exceptions are allowed, but must be approved.

15. The gable end of the principal roof must face the street on which the unit fronts.

16. The required pitch for the principle roof is 6:12. The roof pitch for

ancillary portions of the structure (such as the porch) may vary.

17. Roof shingles must be asphalt; the color is the choice of the client, but must be approved.

### E. EXTERIOR (for all units):

18. Exterior material must be composition board, 4"or 6" lap siding, with wood trim. Exceptions are allowed, but must be approved.

19. Exterior paint color is the choice of the client.

### F. WINDOWS (for all units):

20. Combination living–dining spaces should have 3 windows. Separate living and dining spaces should have 2 windows for each space.

21. The master bedroom in each unit should have 2 windows, preferably providing for cross–ventilation.

22. The secondary bedrooms must have only 1 window each.

23. The bathroom(s) may or may not have windows. This is at the discretion of the client.

### G. TECHNICAL (for all units):

24. HVAC fan units must be attic mounted.

25. Hot water heaters must be attic mounted.

26. Attic access is required, as per code.

27. Roof insulation should be R–26.

28. Wall insulation should be R–11.

29. Each unit should have a closet and the necessary hookups for a side–by–side washer and dryer.

30. All kitchens and bathrooms should be designed for standard modular cabinets, and for standard appliances.

### H. MISCELLANEOUS (for all units):

31. All units are to carpeted throughout, except for sheet vinyl in the kitchen and bathroom(s).

32. Special construction elements, such as bay windows and the like, are discouraged; but, such items may be approved on a case–by–case basis. The criteria for such approvals is the impact of the proposed item on the

construction cost. Proposed items which measurably increase the construction cost will not be approved.

33. Vaulted ceilings in the principle space of the unit may be approved, based on the criteria listed in item 32. In such cases conventional framing or scissors trusses may be employed.

34. Finished floor elevation changes within the unit are permitted upon approval, based on the criteria given in item 32.

## FOR DUPLEX STRUCTURES

35. At least one unit in each duplex structure must be designed for handicapped access, and meet all pertinent handicapped design standards.

36. Duplex structures are to be designed so that one of the units fronts on the main east–west street, and the other unit fronts on the adjacent side street.

# APPENDIX F: CONSTRUCTION CRITICAL PATHS

*The complexity of the BEAT project and the number of people involved made it very difficult to keep everything on schedule. To help with coordination, we developed a series of critical path charts for every home we built. These charts can be created in various popular software packages. Below is a page from one of our charts.*

## Bethel-Ensley Action Task, Inc

## Construction
## Critical Path Chart

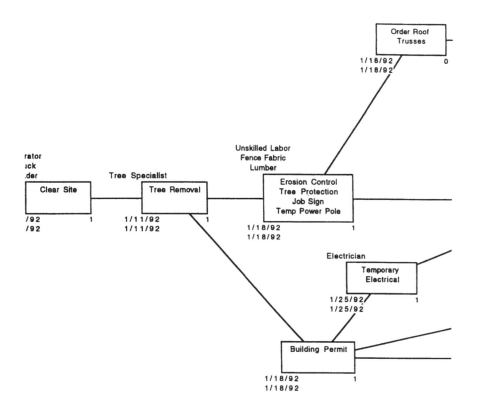

# Appendix G: Community Planning Summaries

*Another part of our planning process was the development of quite detailed summaries of priorities and the steps that would have to be accomplished to fulfill them. We drew up such action summaries in the following areas, each of which had strong committees:*

*Business District*
*Jobs and Economic Development*
*Housing*
*Services and Facilities*
*Youth*
*Environment and Design.*

*On the following pages are examples of the planning summaries.*

# ENSLEY
## COMMUNITY DEVELOPMENT PLAN

### SUMMARY OF EARLY ACTION PRIORITIES & NEXT STEPS

**Environment and Design**

- Support the completion of Village Creek linear park and connect to 19th Street by a landscaped parkway.

- Re-establish Commercial Revitalization District (CRD) in the Business District.

- Initiate plans for the relocation of the salvage yard and extension of open space buffer from Village Creek, west of BEAT development to the Business District.

- Make street infrastructure improvements along Avenue F to Village Creek, on 8th Street between Avenue E and W, along 9th Street between Avenue E and Avenue I, and along 10th Street from Avenue E to Avenue I.

- Improve Interstate edge along Ensley Park by landscaping and screening.

- Establish community gateways at Bush Boulevard, Don Drennen Overpass, and Business District gateways at 20th Street and Avenues E and F.

- Initiate community based clean-up/maintenance program in cooperation with the City to deal with alleys, junk cars, weeds, trash, etc.

- Work with USX to complete environmental assessment and cleanup of Ensley Works Site.

- Work with existing industry and City to clean up industrial sites on edges of neighborhoods.

- Utilize more effective code enforcement to eliminate neighborhood nuisances.

# ENSLEY
## COMMUNITY DEVELOPMENT PLAN

## SUMMARY OF EARLY ACTION PRIORITIES & NEXT STEPS

### Business District

- Support establishment of a Business District Merchants Association and re-establishment of the Commercial Revitalization District (CRD) program.

- Adopt an Urban Development Plan based on the Community Development Plan, with Urban Renewal powers and authority.

- Establish a for-profit and non-profit development agency focusing attention on commercial buildings in and residential areas surrounding the Business District.

- Promote new and renovated retail businesses between Avenues D and G, concentrating on 19th Street. Enhance 18th and 20th Street sides of retail businesses to create "mall-like" effect.

  - Establish target businesses and recruit businesses to locate in this area
  - Establish Historic District by doing historic survey; establish local tax credits for businesses that locate in the Historic District
  - Adopt Business District design guidelines
  - Enforce building codes and CRD codes to the extent possible
  - Provide financial incentives for renovation and to attract new businesses
  - Improve and landscape parking on 20th and 18th Streets to support 19th Street businesses.

- Implement a mixed use retail and One Stop Center Development Project on in a strategic location on 19th Street.

  - Confirm programs for the One Stop
  - Establish agreement with utility companies/other tenants
  - Lease or purchase site
  - Renovations
  - Staffing

- Create a destination restaurant as part of a major development at Avenue E.
  - Recruit restaurant operator
  - arrange financing
  - Assist in acquiring property
  - Assist in renovation/construction

- Undertake a development which includes a first floor upgrade to the Ramsay McCormack Building.

- Implement 19th Street type streetscape along avenues, linking 19th to 20th Street, in conjunction with rehab and development along 19th Street.
  - Extend Avenue E improvements

# ENSLEY
## COMMUNITY DEVELOPMENT PLAN

### SUMMARY OF EARLY ACTION PRIORITIES & NEXT STEPS

#### Jobs and Economic Development

- Increase economic development expertise on ECIF Board and staff
- Establish formal liaison with Metropolitan Development Board (MDB) and the City's Industrial Sites Program.
  - Solicit Ensley property owners to participate in the ECIF
  - Continue visiting local companies to interview owners about plans for expansion and training requirements for employees
- Promote completion of environmental studies and new industrial development of the USX Site.
- Begin to promote industrial and institutional/commercial development of major mixed employment center adjacent to Business District.
- Promote effective job training and new employment in Ensley.
  - Visit job training agencies, vocational schools, JTPA, JOBS, etc. Solicit their participation in the Forum
  - Work with existing companies to form incentives to employ Ensley residents.
  - Create an effective outreach program to get the word out to young people that job training is available.
- Promote projects which will add new jobs/development in the Business District, such as the establishment of the One Stop Service Center.
- Initiate plans and financing for Mixed Use Development at Community Hospital.
- Establish Tuxedo Commercial Revitalization District, including modest street improvements and commercial rehab.
  - Organize owners/businesses
  - Establish district boundaries and guidelines
  - Locate funding and design of improvements
  - Construction of improvements
- Support City's establishment of an outpatient clinic at the old A&P site on 20th Street.
- Utilize 19th Street Merchant's Association, ECIF, Ensley Chamber of Commerce to promote and support existing Ensley businesses.
- Systematically involve elected officials/public agencies in attracting development and jobs to the Ensley Community.
- Extend modest street improvements between Business District and residential areas east and west of 19th Street, and along Avenue E to 24th Street.

# *ENSLEY*
## COMMUNITY DEVELOPMENT PLAN

### SUMMARY OF EARLY ACTION PRIORITIES & NEXT STEPS

#### Housing

- Continue and extend BEAT housing concept toward the Business District and Avenue F, consistent with plans, including land acquisition and street improvements; link into Village Creek Park extension.
  - Acquire lots as needed
  - Make street improvements to connect Sandy Vista to Business District
  - Update BEAT Plan
  - Funding and design of improvements
  - Construction of improvements

- Promote revitalization along major neighborhood corridors such as 14th, 19th, 25th, 31st Streets, and Avenues E, I, L, and Wand as pilot project. Link street improvements, corridors to schools, churches, and parks as framework for parish-like development.
  - Organize residents and landowners
  - Funding and design of improvements
  - Coordinate with housing design

- Initiate plans for major Housing Redevelopment near the Business District and another along 19th and 20th Streets near Tuxedo.

- Include the concept of Assisted Living or comparable facility as part of Community Hospital development (consider alternative site for assisted living if necessary.)

- Complete Village Creek plans and include landscaped parkway; extend park amenities to 18th Street.
  - Work with City and Neighborhoods to identify alternative housing for residents affected by flooding.
  - Follow through with Village Creek Park funding and design improvements

- Utilize effective code enforcement to eliminate neighborhood blighting nuisances
  - Meet with public officials to determine strategy
  - Expedite enforcement of building, zoning, and other codes

- Include housing development financing in non-profit and for-profit development agency; utilize on-going public incentives to finance housing rehab and development.

- ECIF conduct or sponsor an on-going community-based effort to coordinate housing issues and related programs for owners, renters, and developers; issues include responsible ownership and responsible tenants, and workshops on educational and financial strategies.

# ENSLEY
## COMMUNITY DEVELOPMENT PLAN

### SUMMARY OF EARLY ACTION PRIORITIES & NEXT STEPS

**Services and Facilities**

- Initiate plans with Western Health Center and others to expand Health Care and related services to include Day Care.
  - Work with health care providers to determine exactly what services are currently offered, hours of operation, types of payment accepted, etc.
  - Inform health care providers about the kind of care Ensley residents are seeking and as them to help locate these kind of providers
  - Determine how health care system can focus on preventative, family-oriented medicine
  - Reinforce presence of the Western Health Center

- Support City's establishment of an outpatient clinic at the former A&P site on 20th Street.

- Explore the possibility of developing a Cooper Green Hospital Community Care Clinic in Ensley.

- Develop short-term improvements which will enhance transit service through MAX or an alternate Jitney/Shuttle service.

- Operate a One Stop Center as Service Delivery improvement as part of mixed use development on 19th Street.

- Merchants and Community leaders work more closely to increase use of Police Precinct as community asset.
  - Increase police presence in patrol cars, on foot, and on bicycle.
  - Increase visibility of Ensley Police station.
  - Meet regularly with Police Chief and Mayor.

- Develop specific programs to maximize job training centers at Jackson Olin, Ensley High School, and JCCEO and other non-profit entities.

- Complete Village Creek plans to increase community recreation services.

- Establish well-organized community based cleanup and maintenance program, using sub-districts created by the Plan as an organizing principle.

- Utilize community-based organization to coordinate housing issues and related programs for owners, renters, and developers. Include components on responsibilities of owning and renting and workshops and other educational strategies on financing

# Index